Faith Flowers
LAURA IAROCCI

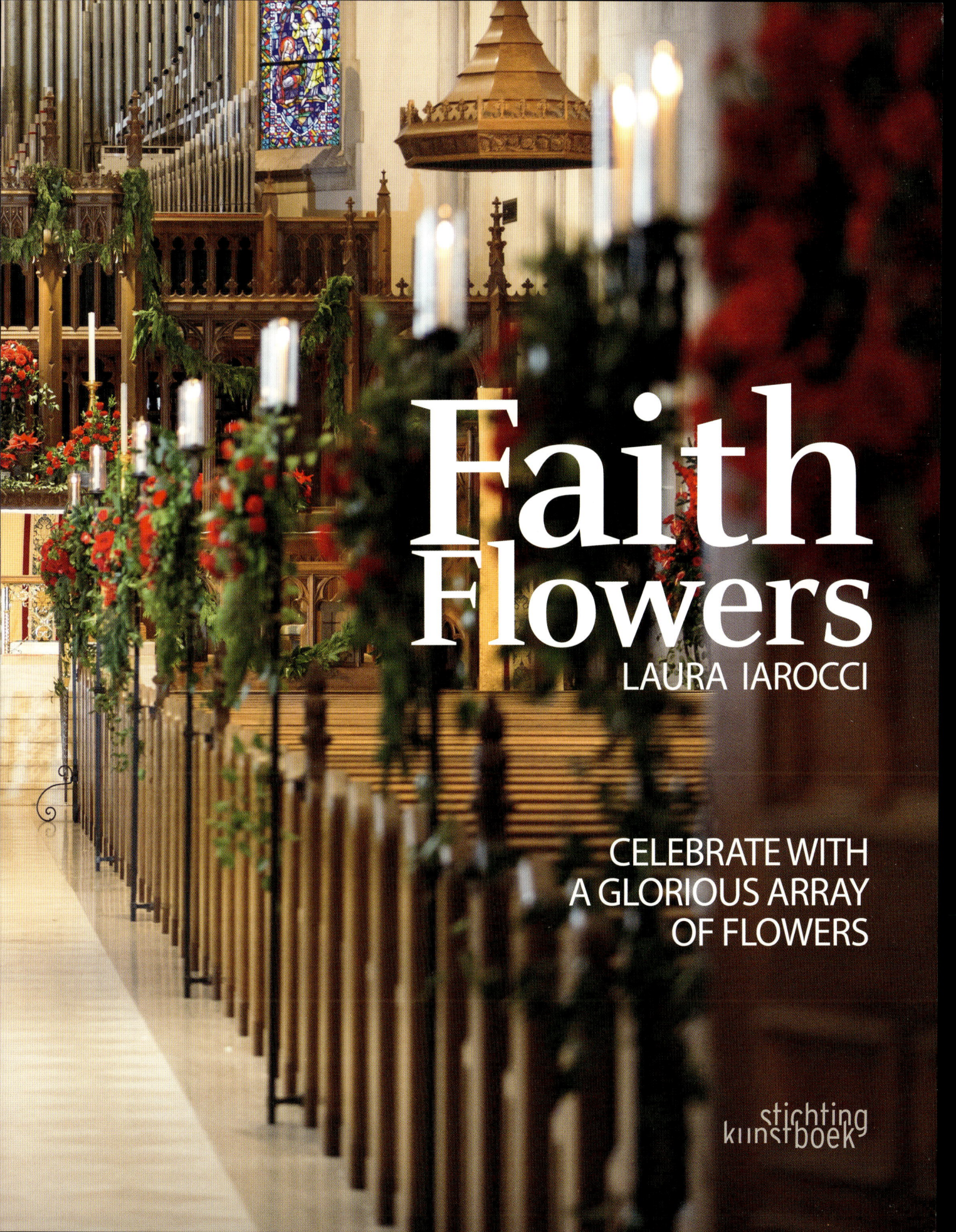

Faith Flowers
LAURA IAROCCI

CELEBRATE WITH A GLORIOUS ARRAY OF FLOWERS

stichting kunstboek

Contents

My Story	p.6
About this book	p.8

The Basics
Church Flower Principles	p.10
Funding Church Flowers	p.11
What is a Flower Guild	p.12
Planning the Flowers	p.14
Color Guide	p.16
How to Buy Flowers	p.18
Conditioning Flowers	p.20
Basic Supplies	p.22
Containers	p.24
Your Church Garden	p.26
My favorite greenery	p.28

Basic Techniques
The Support Structure	p.30
Wiring and more	p.32

Basic Designs
Classic Triangle	p.34
Floral Sprays	p.36
Wreaths	p.38
Garland	p.40
Moss Crosses	p.42
Topiaries	p.44

Church Flower Designs
Sunday
Introduction	p.46
Grand Classic Triangle	p.48
Classic Triangle with Hydrangea	p.50
Classic Triangle Two Ways	p.51
Monochromatic	p.52
Caroline's Cascade	p.53
Mary and Martha	p.54
Golden Garden Greenery	p.55
From the Garden	p.56
Moongate	p.58
Summer Sunflowers	p.60
Dramatic Summer Garden	p.62
Small Garden Compote	p.64
Potted Composition	p.66
Winter Wonderland	p.67
Garden Altar	p.68
Pumpkin Stacks	p.70
Summer Fun	p.71

Weddings
Introduction	p.72
Classic Wedding Urns	p.74
Hydrangea Orb	p.76
Small Design Concepts	p.77
Radial Designs	p.78
A Garden Altar	p.80
Iron Stands	p.81
Sophie's Garden Wedding	p.82
A Spring Fresh Wedding	p.84
Wedding Wreaths	p.86
Pew Sprays	p.88

Christmas
Introduction	p.90
Christmas and Advent Greenery	p.92
Christmas Special Flowers	p.93
Advent Wreath	p.94
Advent Altar	p.96
Main Altar	p.98
Classic Christmas Altar	p.100
Window Box	p.101
Floral Sprays	p.102
Wreaths	p.104
Draping Ivy Wall	p.106

Easter
Introduction	p.108
Main Altar	p.110
Garden Altar Base	p.112
Door or Column Baskets	p.114
Pulpit	p.116
Flowering Cross	p.118
Kneeling Altar	p.119
Garland	p.120
Processional Cross	p.122
Paschal Candle	p.123

Other Festival Days
Introduction	p.124
Pentecost: Altar of Flames	p.126
Pentecost: Single Design	p.127
Funerals: On the Wings of Angels	p.128
Baptism	p.130
Thanksgiving	p.131

Receptions
Introduction	p.132
Grande Urn	p.134
Small Centrepiece	p.136
Blush Centerpiece	p.138

Flower Festivals	p.140
Thanks and Acknowledgements	p.142
Imprint	p.144

"Though I do not believe that a plant will spring up where no seed has been, I have great faith in a seed. Convince me that you have a seed there, and I am prepared to expect wonders."

Henry D. Thoreau

My story

Being involved with my church Flower Guild has been one of the highlights of my life. The quiet joy of arranging flowers behind the scenes has been part of my routine for over 20 years. (Sometimes the organist rehearsing reduced the silence but increased the joy!)

When my children were little, it was a welcome moment of peace in the chaos of the week. As I have grown older, arranging flowers still brings me peace. But, it is also my way to remain a part of the life of my church as we play our part in making each Sunday service, funeral or wedding more beautiful. Arranging flowers is like prayer. It's a way to worship God while creating art. And, it has been a special way to connect with fellow parishioners.

Before I started my floral work at church, my only connection with flowers was that I loved them and wanted to learn more about them. Up until that point, I had been a Wall Street banker.

I longed for a creative outlet. I had recently moved back to Atlanta and was looking for a way to get reconnected in my home church. A friend asked me to join the Flower Guild at the Episcopal Cathedral of St. Philip. I went to a demonstration in Atlanta by Sheila McQueen, the grand dame of English flowers, and was hooked. I wanted to learn everything I could about arranging flowers. There were not so many flower arranging classes then as there are today. A very kind gentleman named Tyler Gresham, whose family had owned a flower shop in Atlanta, took me under his wing when I became the Flower Guild chair. He taught me how to buy flowers, prepare recipes and design in the classic English style. I worked as much as possible with the many other experienced arrangers on the Flower Guild. I set about taking as many classes as I could find.
Over time, I have taken classes with some of the leading designers and instructors in the world. Each year, I lead floral tours to Europe, which continue to expose me to a host of new designs and ideas that I apply in church design.

In 2010, I started a floral design studio called 'Faith Flowers'. I chose that name because my life with flowers sprang from my faith in God which, in turn, led me to get involved with our Flower Guild. The role of faith in all that I do has deepened over the years. Faith is what leads our guild members to dedicating so much of their time to creating beautiful flowers week in and week out. When the days and nights are long and full of flower worries, I have faith that God will provide and get us through all that is before us. I took a leap of faith when we sold our house and leased a studio space for the business. The Faith Flowers studio now includes a flower school, flower tours around the world and floral design for weddings, events and funerals. The book title is a natural extension of our studio name. I hope that your faith will lead you to a greater exploration of the world of flowers too as you read this book and experience the joy of working with flowers.

About This Book

I wrote this book to make church flower arranging accessible to all and so that others may know the joy of working with flowers. The book is written in a very basic step-by-step format so that a beginner can follow along. It is meant to be opened up and spread out on a counter while working.

Over the years, I have taught hundreds of people church flower arranging. I have included answers to the many questions people ask starting with what is Oasis? How is the best way to condition Roses? Why do my Hydrangea wilt? I have included recipes for each arrangement because I know that is what I wanted to know when I started ordering flowers

My church background is in the Anglican tradition, which has a rich appreciation for flowers in worship spaces. No doubt, this stems from the special English love of flowers. But, I have worked with churches of varying denominations and sizes. I have an appreciation for the role and demands of flowers in churches large and small.

We all struggle to create beautiful flowers, often with limited budgets and with volunteer labor. This book is designed to help people learn the basics of flower arranging that can apply to a variety of spaces and church traditions

The book begins with the principles of church flower designs. We have also included information on how to start and manage a flower guild at your church, which is based upon my own experiences and from the other churches I have worked with over the years.

In The Basics section, we cover the fundamentals of flower arranging in churches. I have included practical information on how to plan, order, fund and buy flowers. Color ideas and liturgical color information are provided.

The steps for conditioning flowers, which is the key to beautiful flowers, follow. This section also includes a description of flower arranging supplies and garden materials.

The Third section of the book includes step-by-step instructions for a variety of designs. Each design has a recipe showing all the ingredients needed. The recipes will give you a basis for ordering your own flowers. The designs start with a basic design section showing how to create the most commonly used arrangements in church flower design.

The next designs illustrate a variety of flower arrangements that can be used on Sundays throughout the year.

The instructions begin with simple designs and continue on to more advanced large-scale designs. Design ideas and techniques for the holiest celebrations are highlighted in separate sections on Christmas and Easter. Other special festival designs are covered as well. A special section on Weddings includes photographs from real weddings.

This book concludes with a section on Flower Festivals.

I recognize that the use of flowers in churches varies considerably among denominations and individual churches. Flower arrangements can range from a very simple basket of flowers to classic urns to expansive festival altars.

While floral practices vary church-to-church, the presence of flowers is always warmly received. Church flower designs may be created by volunteers or professionals or a combination of both. I am sure everyone will enjoy this book no matter the denomination or church affiliation. I wrote this book because I believe that anyone who has the desire to create flowers for his or her own church should be able to do so.

The Basics   Church Flower Principles

All glory be to God ~
Flowers are created to the glory of god.
We create floral designs in church spaces to glorify God. A glorious array of flowers is one of God's greatest creations.

Flowers should lead the eye to the cross.
For church spaces with central crosses or crucifixes, the floral designs should lead the eye to the cross to focus on the centrality of Jesus.

Flowers should enhance not overwhelm the worship space.
Flowers are meant to enhance the worship experience and church space. The flowers are not meant to be a centerpiece as they would be at a party.

Flowers should not go above the arms of the cross.
If the floral arrangements are too large they will overpower the cross.

Flowers are reflective of God's creation: Use natural elements and seasonally available flowers.
Flowers are a physical expression of the glory of God's creations. Churches should use real flowers and greenery, which God has provided us in nature. Bringing the outside inside softens and makes a sacred space more alive. Some of the most effective designs use flowers and greenery from arrangers or parishioners' yards. Get creative with what God has provided us!

Placement and viewpoint guide the design.
Individual churches have particular spatial considerations which must be taken into account when planning the flowers. Where will the flowers be placed? Are the designs in a central point or off to the side?
Is there one design or two in the space? The point of view of the flowers is critical to planning floral designs. Will the flowers be viewed up close or will most people look at the flowers from afar?

Follow your church color guidelines.
Using seasonally available flowers marks the different seasons of nature and compliment the church calendar.

Functionality of designs.
Know how your church services flow so that the flowers are not in the way of the clergy or parishioners. Make sure flowers are placed so that there is clear access for all to move around. An arrangement could come tumbling forward or branches could catch on the robe of a priest. (If you are not careful, it happens!)

Reverence.
Church flower arrangers have a special privilege of working in sacred spaces. One should be respectful a nd reverent when working in altar areas.

Cleanliness is next to godliness.
A good amount of humility is involved in arranging flowers in a church space. As often as we are arranging flowers, we are also on the floor picking up flower debris or cleaning buckets. Cleaning up makes everyone's work easier.

Each church has its own special traditions and flower requirements.
Consult with your clergy about what they want regarding the flowers. Flowers can vary parish-to-parish and clergy-to-clergy. Also there may be special days to be celebrated in each parish such as patron feast days.

Flowers are an individual expression of love for God and fellow parishioners.
Each flower arrangement is a unique and sacred expression of the person creating it. Flower arranging, in a manner of speaking, is prayer. In the act of arranging, we put something of ourselves into the creation and offer both – flowers and self – to the glory of God.

Funding Church Flowers

Flowers in churches are typically paid for largely through donations from parishioners in memory or in honor of or in thanksgiving for loved ones and friends. Donations are collected for Sunday flowers and during specials seasons, particularly for Christmas and Easter. Fees are charged for flowers for weddings and funerals. Rarely is there room in a church budget to fund the cost of flowers.

Tips on Donations

- Have a clear method on the website to make donations specifically for flowers.
- Place Flower Donation forms in the central area of the church.
- Set up a table to collect donations during Advent and Lent and periodically throughout the year. Have photos of prior years' flowers.
- Allow more than one donation each week.
- Many churches have a tradition of asking for donations for Easter Lilies or Christmas Poinsettias. Collect funds instead for "Easter Flowers" and "Christmas Flowers" which expands the types of flowers used.

Charges for Flowers:
Fees should be charged for flowers for weddings, funerals and any other special events hosted at the church. The fees should cover the cost of the flowers and materials used. They should also include funds to cover the general maintenance, operation, training and purchases of the Flower Guild. A detailed list of flower fees should be prepared to include the following. Consider offering two levels such as "Classic or Grand Arrangements" or "Small or Large".

- Wedding Altar Flowers
- Pew Sprays
- Floral Wreaths
- Funeral Flowers Fees
- Funeral Reception Centerpieces

Other ways to raise money:
- Offer additional options for weddings such as aisle candles. A fee for using the aisle candles should be charged.
- Host a Flower Festival or Flower Demonstration: Invite parishioners and the greater community to attend for a fee.
- The Flower Guild can do extra flowers for weddings such as pew sprays, wreaths, garlands, or pedestals.

The Basics

What is a Flower Guild

How do they work?

A Flower Guild is a simply a team of people who work together to arrange the flowers for a church. In the middle ages, a "guild" was an association of craftsmen.

The purpose of a Flower Guild is:
1. Glorify God through creating flower arrangements for religious spaces and services.
2. Enhance the worship experience for all involved.
3. Remind others of beauty as a reflection of God's creation.
4. Provide fellowship, support and training among guild members.

I am convinced that parishioners can and should arrange the flowers in churches. Parishioners arrange the flowers with more love and care than a commercial florist. They add special touches from their gardens and labor to make it just right. Because donations can go towards the purchase of flowers and materials, churches can have better quality flowers. The better the flowers look, the more flower donations will grow. Generally, flower guilds are open to all members of parish who are willing to arrange flowers on a regular basis and to be part of training. Our church has non-parishioners as well. Members usually serve on a volunteer basis. Guild members can include novices to professionals and all skill levels in between. Indeed, a range of abilities is needed as there are very basic tasks to more complicated ones requiring advanced skills levels. Flower Guilds pull from a wide range of a church membership. The common uniting interest is flowers. Friendships are formed when working together to create flower arrangements.

How do you start a new Flower Guild or revive one?
A great way is to host a flower arranging demonstration and invite the members of the parish and others to attend. Some churches start on a limited basis arranging flowers once a month, adding more Sundays as new members are recruited. Florists can deliver the flowers on alternate weeks. New Flower Guild members can be recruited in a variety of ways. A flower demonstration or workshop to teach beginners is one of the best ways to obtain and train new members. This workshop can be conducted by a member of the Flower Guild or an outside instructor. Advertise periodically in church newsletters for new members. Ask Guild members to invite their friends to join. Visit different church groups offering a slide presentation or a flower arranging demonstration.
There is always someone who is curious to learn how to arrange flowers and is looking for a way to connect.

How to structure a flower guild?
There are a number of options for structuring a Flower Guild. Knowing your parish is the best way to determine how to make it work.

Here are some models:
1. Two teams with two Co-Chairs with alternating months of responsibility or differing jobs.
2. Four different teams responsible for one Sunday per month (i.e. First Sunday of the month).
3. One Chair who makes assignments on an as available basis each month.
4. Flower Guild and Professional: Flower guilds arrange the flowers once or twice a month and hire professionals for the other weeks or special occasions.

Flower Guild Leadership
Flower Guilds thrive with great leadership. They are servant-leaders. The best qualities for Flower Guild leaders are humility, dedication and organization. They focus on the church and the people they serve. They are continuous learners who are committed to the growth and development of everyone around them. Strong organizational skills are needed to put together volunteer schedules and flower orders.

As the role is typically volunteer, the Flower Guild Chair responsibilities are best divided between at least two people. Build upon the personal skills of the chairs. One chair could order flowers and the other organize the volunteers.

The Flower Guild Chair assures that flowers are placed as needed for each week. To make this happen, the chair sets the schedules for volunteer and professional flower arrangers. The chairs are responsible for making sure the flowers are ordered for weekly and special flowers. They also make sure that the budget and arranging guidelines are followed. They should also plan for the training of the team and new members.

Flower Guild leaders can be trained to plan and order flowers. Ideally Flower Guild leaders should have some experience in selecting and ordering flowers. They could be professional florists, but they need not be professionals. Working as a shadow assisting a current leader is a good way to learn. Attending flower arranging classes is also helpful. A well-developed set of flower recipes for basic altar arrangements is a critical planning tool. Historical recipes and photographs are good guides as the seasons progress. In some churches, each team selects its flowers which is also a good way to build flower ordering skills of several people.

The weekly schedule of a Flower Guild?
Each church will develop its own schedule based upon its guild members and church schedule. See on the right a basic schedule of a Flower Guild for each week.

Weekly Flower Guild Schedule

When	What
Week Before	Pre-Order Flowers
Monday/Tuesday	Select Flowers from Wholesaler
Wednesday/Thursday	Condition Flowers
Friday/Saturday	Teams meet to arrange flowers
Saturday/Sunday/Tuesday	Water flowers
Sunday/Monday/Friday	Breakdown Flowers

What happens to flowers after Sunday services?

The answer depends upon the practices of individual churches. Some churches are active during the week. They typically leave the flowers up for the entire week for people coming to worship during the week. Team members for the following week can break them down. Some churches break them down on Sunday or Monday to deliver to ill parishioners or to use in staff offices. Make sure the flowers are in good condition if doing so.

Flower Guild Chair Calendar

This calendar outlines the basic responsibilities for Flower Guild Chairs set by month. The calendar should be amended to add preparations for any special days for particular churches.

Monthly:
- Set schedule for next month looking closely at special services or instructions for that month.
- Send Flower Guild members request for availability at least 30 days prior to the next month.
- Order and select flowers as needed.
- Contact brides sixty days in advance regarding flower selection and extra flower requests.
- Track basic flower arranging supplies. Watch wholesaler's good sales.

September:
- Begin planning Christmas.
- Hold a fall Flower Guild meeting.

October: Christmas Pre-orders are typically due at end of October
- Order wreaths, greenery, garland and Poinsettias.
- Buy fall items including leaves, gourds, pumpkins and interesting squashes.

November:
- Make plan and start Christmas flower donation requests in bulletins and in person.
- Thanksgiving altar.
- Set up Advent wreaths for first Sunday in Advent
- Store all fall dried goods.

December:
- Collect Christmas flower donations.
- Send out volunteer request forms for Christmas decorations and clean up.
- Order Christmas flowers.
- Clean up Christmas (depending upon custom).

January:
- Organize Christmas clean up: after Epiphany or earlier.
- Order any red Roses or flowers needed for Valentine's weekend.

Lent: (February to April depending upon date of Easter)
- Make plan, start Easter flower donation requests in bulletins and in person.
- Plan Palm Sunday and Easter.
- Order Easter Lilies.
- Prepare Palm Sunday and Easter orders.
- Clean cabinets and storage areas thoroughly.

March/April:
- Palm Sunday
- Easter preparations

May:
- Order Mother's Day Flowers early.
- Determine if special services need flowers such as graduations, etc.

Summer Months: When many volunteers are on vacation
- Organize schedules in advance.
- Consider alternative arrangements that last multiple weeks such as potted compositions.

The Basics

Planning The Flowers

There is definitely an art and science to planning and buying flowers. Planning your flowers ahead of time is the first step. As you buy the flowers week in and week out, you will develop a better sense of what works together, what works best in your space, and availability at your wholesaler.

Step 1 Consider Your Space

The first most important step is to think about where the flowers will be placed.

1. **What size design to do you need?** You do not want the flowers to overwhelm the space or conversely be too small. Select a container and flowers that fit your space in terms of size and color.
2. **How far back will the arrangement be placed from the viewer?** If the arrangement will be placed far back from the congregation, as it is in many churches, larger blooms and stronger colors will show better. Small delicate flowers and berries will not show and are a waste of money.
3. **What color is the background?** Colors show up very well against a white background. White will disappear unless you use plenty of greenery to break it up. Similarly, if the background is wood, brown tones and some green ones will not show well.

Step 2 Plan Your Basic Flower Recipes

The flower selection starts with the planning. The first step is to determine the basic flowers needed for each area you are going to decorate. Create a "Recipe" as you would for cooking. Break the flowers and greenery into general categories of flowers organized by their role in a design. Here are the basic categories. Examples are listed for each type. Be creative – there are many other flowers in each category. Many flowers fit a couple of categories:

Line: Linear flowers set the outer shape of a design. More limited options exist for line flowers.
Examples: Snapdragons, Gladiolas, Larkspur, Delphinium, Bells of Ireland, Millet, Blooming Branches.

Focal Flowers: Larger blooms are the most important ones in a design. Focal flowers are often the most expensive blooms. They are placed in the area of focal emphasis where the eye is drawn to in a design.
Examples: Roses, Peonies, Lilies, Spider Mums, Dahlias, Garden Roses, Amaryllis.

Supporting Blooms: Like a supporting actor or actress they support the color and shape of the focal flower.
Examples: Carnations, Spray Carnations, Tulips, Spray Roses, Hydrangea, Roses.

Filler: Flowers that help fill the space and provide emphasis or contrast to the main flowers.
Examples: Waxflower, Baby's Breath, Queen Anne's Lace, Mums, Orlaya, Limonium.

Line Greenery: Linear greenery helps set the shape of the design. Not always needed but is a nice addition if available.
Examples: Myrtle, Sasanqua, Italian Ruscus, Leucothoe, Elaeagnus, Baby Blue Eucalyptus, Holly Fern, Abelia.

Base Greenery: Basic greenery covers the Oasis and fills an arrangement. Examples: Pittosporum, Leather Leaf, Salal

Accent Greenery: Greenery that adds a special touch emphasizing a color like Sage Green or providing a contrasting texture. Often added last. Garden greenery works well. Optional.
Examples: Seeded Eucalyptus, Dusty Miller, Boxwood

Special Material: Sometimes there is something special in the cooler or something blooming locally that adds that special touch to an arrangement to make it sing!

Basic Recipes: How Many Flowers Do You Need?:
The important thing is to know **how many** of each type you need for your design. That will help keep you in budget. Here are some sample "Recipes". To minimize leftovers, we have designed these recipes to work with bunch sizes of 10 stems per bunch for most flowers. Roses are typically 12 per bunch at the grocery store and 25 per bunch from the wholesaler.
We have listed flowers needed by the stem except for filler flowers and greenery which come in varying sizes of stems per bunch. If you use a pair of arrangements, multiply the recipes by two. They should work well with one bunch of wholesale Roses. You will find lots of recipes throughout this book. These will get you started.
Develop basic recipes for your own spaces.
Keep them with you when you order and select flowers.

Single Arrangement for Small Altar

7-10	Stems	Line Flowers
5-6	Stems	Focal Flowers
3-6	Stems	Supporting Flowers
1	Bunch	Filler Flower
1	Bunch	Basic Greenery

Add an additional bunch of line or contrasting greenery budget permitting or find something from the garden.

Single Arrangement for Large Altar

1-2	Bunches	Line Flowers
6-12	Stems	Focal Flowers (depending on size)
5-12	Stems	Supporting Flowers
2	Bunches	Filler Flower
1	Bunch	Line Greenery
2	Bunch	Basic Greenery

Add an additional bunch of line or contrasting greenery budget permitting.

Hint
When first starting to buy flowers, go to the wholesaler or grocery store. **Experiment!** Pull different flowers and colors to see how they look together.

Flower Facts

Bunch sizes — **Stems per Bunch**
- Most Flowers — 10
- Roses — 25 Wholesale / 12 Grocery Store
- Mums — 6-8
- Filler & Greenery — Varies based on volume

Step 3
Select your color palette:
See the following section on Color.
Take these colors inspirations and determine your color palette.

Step 4
Determine Flowers for Each Color by Flower Type:
- Look at what is blooming or in season in your area.
- Visit your local wholesaler or grocery store.
- Use online Flower Galleries such as www.cutflower.com
- Google images
- Create your own Flower Gallery listings of favorite flowers
- Pull flowers to see what works well together.

Step 5
Write the recipe for the flowers you have ordered by area. Samples of flower recipes can be found throughout the book

Advanced Flower Planning Techniques:
When you are planning flowers for multiple altars, spaces or festivals, a spread sheet should be prepared to plan the flowers. These calculations can be done by hand but are much simpler and more accurate when a spreadsheet is used. When planning larger sets of festival flowers such as Christmas and Easter, a spreadsheet is invaluable. It is best to start learning on the simple weekly flower orders.

We also use a Flower Planning program called *Details Flowers*. This program allows floral designers to create individual flower recipes and flower orders, project expenses, track flower costs, select flowers from its flower gallery, and show flower photos to your Flower Guild. Prior recipes can be saved which is enormously helpful when planning.

Information on *Details Flowers* is located in www.detailsflowers.com. In general, organize the flowers by color and type to make sure there is enough of each one. This also helps so that you can sum the totals of each stem and make sure you are using as many of the stems ordered as possible. Order a few extra stems to allow for breakage or other problems. Try to break the flowers into groupings that correspond with the number of stems typically contained in each bunch. This will keep you from having too many extra flowers.

The Basics

God created a myriad of flower color combinations to choose between.

One of the joys of choosing flowers for your church is getting to see how different colors work in your church. Don't be afraid to try new color combinations. Take notes on what looks best in your space with the lighting and the background of the walls and floors.

Here are some ways to find inspiration or guidance to get started selecting your flower color palette. Use one of these color ideas to build your color palette:
- If applicable, start with the Liturgical Color for your church (See Liturgical Color Chart).
- Look around at what is blooming or in season in your area.
- Go to your wholesaler or grocery store to see what is in season and beautiful.
- Look at wholesalers online listings or videos of available flowers.
- Find out what is on sale at your wholesaler.
- Use the colors in a multi-colored Rose or Tulip as a starting point.
- Look in books, magazines and on the internet for floral designs you like and note the color combination. It does not have to be a church design.
- If there is a wedding, find out the color palette and flowers.
- See our list of possible color combinations.
- Join the Faith Flowers Guild and watch the weekly postings from different churches.

Flower Color Combination Options:

Monochromatic:
Try staying within one color.
You will be surprised how much variation there can be within the same color. Different flowers of the same color can provide interesting texture contrasts.

All yellow * All green * All orange * All pink * All white

Analogous Color:
Colors within a range of adjacent hues

light orange to deep red

yellow to orange to red

pink to purple

yellow to green

Color Guide

Some of our Favorite Color Combinations:

White * Blue * Green :

        Alternative: Add yellow or purple

White * Ivory * Green

Orange * Purple * Green:
    "Secondary" Colors

Ivory * Burgundy * Pink * Grey * Sage Green

Yellow * White

Pink * Peach * Pale Yellow

Deep Pink * Soft Pink * Ivory *

Liturgical Colors

Seasons in the church are marked by the use of different colors. This chart generally describes the colors of the seasons in some churches. There may be special customs in different areas or parishes. The color refers to the color of the vestments and paraments that are used on each occasion. The flower colors should complement and enhance this color. It does not mean that the flowers have to be exclusively this color.
See color shedule on right page.

Flower Fact

Deep purple and dark blue are receding colors and will disappear in large church spaces creating black spots in a design.

Season	Period	Color	Church
Season of Christmas	December 25 to January 5th	White White - Gold Red	Presbyterian Traditional
Season after Epiphany	January 6 to Lent 1st Sunday after Epiphany	Green White	
Lent	Ash Wednesday to Easter	Purple	
Laetere Sunday	1th Sunday in Lent	Pink	Catholic
Palm Sunday	Sunday before Easter	Purple Red	Protestant Catholic
Holy Week		Red	
Maundy Thursday		Purple Altar stipped: no color or flowers	
Good Friday		Purple No color	
Easter		White - Gold White	Catholic/Presbyterian Methodist/Episcopal
Pentecost	50 days after Easter	Red	
"Ordinary Time"	After Pentecost Sunday to Advent	Green: meaning any colors	
All Saints Day	November 1 or 1st Sunday November	White	
Advent		Purple Purple or Royal Blue	Catholic
Gadette Sunday	3rd Sunday Advent	Pink	Catholic
Christmas	12 days of Christmas	White White - Gold	Catholic/Presbyterian
Ordinations		Red	
Feast of Martyrs		Red	Catholic
Feast of Mary & Non Martyr Saints		White	Catholic
Replace red, green or white		Gold	Catholic
Funerals		White	
Marriages		White	

The Basics   How to Buy Flowers

Who Buys Flowers?
Different churches handle the purchasing of flowers in different ways. In some churches the people who are arranging flowers purchase the flowers. They are given a budget for the flowers. Some churches have teams that arrange flowers each week. They often have an experienced team leader who can select the flowers. The model that we use in our Cathedral is that Flower Guild Co-Chairs plan and select the flowers each week. We take turns in alternating months so it is not overwhelming. In larger churches this is the most economic and efficient method.

Where do you buy flowers?
The ideal place to buy flowers is at a local wholesaler where one can look at the flowers and pull different combinations. When learning to buy flowers, going to the wholesaler is the best way to begin, even if it means driving a distance. Many churches are not near major wholesalers or ones that provide a broad range of product. There are many reputable on line floral wholesalers that can deliver flowers to the church via truck or overnight air.

Where to Buy Flowers?
- Local Wholesaler
- Online Wholesaler
- Grocery Store
- Local farms or farmers markets)

Developing a good relationship with a wholesaler is key. They can give you advice on types of flowers, cost and methods of handling flowers. Learn your wholesalers ordering system to find out when orders are due.

Often wholesalers offer promotional programs to encourage early orders and the sale of specific flowers which may be in season. Sometimes a good way to start planning your weekly flowers is to find out what is on sale.

Other options include grocery or big box stores which are offering an ever-increasing array of floral products. Check with your local store to find out when they receive flowers and whether you can order in advance. For smaller churches the advantage of buying from grocery stores is that you can get Roses in smaller quantities usually one dozen. Farmers markets have an abundance of beautiful local flowers and are becoming more prevalent. Find out where and when your local farmers markets are held. Your choice will be limited to what is in season, but sometimes that can be fun. As you get to know the farmers, you will also learn what is being grown.

How much do they cost?
Flower costs have risen significantly as wages and transportation costs have increased. The prices vary between wholesalers and are based upon your location and other factors. Distance from the flower field is one factor. For example, the cost of flowers in California where the majority of flowers are grown in the U.S. is significantly less than on the East Coast.

Determine a budget with pricing from your market. After creating your Basic Flower Recipes, price the list with your supplier to find out the average cost of those types of stems. Figure out what your basic budget should be by multiplying the number of stems by the average cost. Figure in that special weeks with weddings may be more expensive. Make a spread sheet and track the actual prices over time. If you use a flower ordering program like Details Flowers, you can track the weekly price in that program. You can also insert the projected costs to see what your plan is costing.

What to buy?
- Flowers with bright fresh-looking green leaves
- Firm blooms that are not fully open
- Local, in-season flowers
- 3 to 5 different types
- Contrasting shapes and textures

What not to buy?
- Flowers with browned edges
- Flowers with limp heads
- Flowers with slimy leaves
- Flowers with leaves falling off
- Flowers that have been in the cooler over a week

When to buy flowers?
Planning ahead is critical to having the freshest flowers and flowers that are opened perfectly for the day you need them. When ordering flowers, it is generally best to order them two weeks in advance of the date you will be using them. Find out the ordering deadline for your wholesalers. If you are selecting from the wholesaler or another store, find out when they receive their flowers. You should buy them within a day or two of arrival. For example, the wholesalers we work with typically get their flowers over the weekend and put them in the cooler on Monday and Tuesday. Those days are the best days to select them.

The Basics Conditioning your flowers

The key to having the most beautiful flowers is to conditioning them well. You need to have the knowledge and take the time to get them to open properly. howing up with flowers in wrappers and arranging right away will not produce beautiful or long lasting flowers. These are the techniques we have used in processing thousands of stems weekly.

How to condition flowers

1. Start with a clean bucket: All buckets should be scrubbed and washed with soap and water or floral cleaner. A textured sponge or dish brush work well for scrubbing.
2. Fill buckets half way with room temperature water.
3. Add flower conditioner. Be sure to follow quantity instructions on container.
4. Remove all wrappers.
5. Strip leaves off most flowers, especially greenery which will be underwater.
6. Cut at an angle with sharp scissors, garden clippers or knife and make sure the cutting tools are sharp so that they do not crush the cells. It will also make the cutting go much faster.
7. Dip for 2 to 3 seconds in Quick Dip.
8. Place in a bucket filled half way with room temperature water.

Exceptions to the Rules:
1. Remove outer leaves on Tulips. Rewrap with wrappers for storage in cooler.
2. Soft stemmed flowers like Tulips, Calla Lilies, Ranunculus and Gerbera:
    a. Do not like a lot of water. 3" is enough.
    b. Do not dip these in hydra quick, the stems will be burned.

Tips and tricks

1. For very tight flowers, place in very warm water. Recut daily and put in warm water.
2. Do not overcrowd buckets. Flowers need room to open. Spread out through the bucket.

3. Do not leave in direct sunlight.
4. White, Cream or Light Pink flowers bruise easily. Do not lay them down. Place in one bucket, cut and put in another bucket.
5. Be careful not to drip water on blooms.

Time needed to condition

We have prepared a chart which shows the approximate time to get many commonly used flowers open. The chart also shows which flowers do best when refrigerated. Refrigeration depends on your climate.

The first step is to know WHEN you need the flowers opened. If you have a wedding on Saturday, you want them to be open and perfect for the wedding.
They will last until Sunday if they are conditioned well. If you need them for Sunday, gear your timing towards Sunday.

If you want them to last for a long time, condition them for 24 hours and then arrange. They will continue to open and change in the Oasis.

Our prepping philosophy is "When in doubt test it out!". A couple of weeks ahead, try new flowers or garden materials you are not familiar with. See how they do in or out of the cooler. Test whether they like Oasis.
It will save heartache later!

Conditioning Time Chart

Commonly Used Church Flowers
Before Beginning Your Conditioning
1. Know what state of opening your flowers typically arrive in.
   (I.e. Are the Alstroemeria tight or open).
2. Temperature of room where flowers will be stored.
   (Ours is fairly warm so many flowers must be put in cooler).
3. "When in doubt, test it out".

Flower		Days to open	Storage
Alstroemeria		3 to 6	Room Temperature
Carnations		2 to 4	Gently rub to open
Chrysanthemums	Button	3 to 5	Room Temperature
	Cushion	1 to 2	Room Temperature
Dahlias		1 day	Cooler
Delphinium		1 to 3	Leave out if tight
Eucalyptus		Ready to go	Cooler
Gerbers		Ready to go	Cooler
Gladiolas		3 to 5	Room Temperature
Greenery		Ready to go	Most Greenery with exceptions can be left out
Hydrangea	Most Lt. Pink	1 to 2	Room Temperature Store in Cooler
Iris		1 day	Room Temperature
Larkspur		1 day	Cooler: Remove most side shoots
Leather Leaf		Ready to go	Spray with water and store in bag in cooler
Lilies		3 to 5	Room Temperature
Roses	Dry Pack	2 to 4	Leave in cardboard. Fresh cut and leave in water for a few hours. Then process.
	White	3 to 5	Room Temperature
	Orange	1 to 2	Room Temperature
	Others	2 to 4	Room Temperature
	Garden	2 to 4	Store in cooler for 24 hours. Then Process
Salal		Ready to go	Spray with water and store in bag in cooler
Snapdragons		1 day	Cooler
Spray Roses		1 to 2	Cooler
Stock		Ready to go	Cooler

The Basics
Basic Supplies

Strainer — To catch pieces of flower debris, leaves and berries when emptying buckets

Sprayer

Cake Turntable — For heavy containers

Plastic Stands — To hold flower recipes or instructions

Turntables in varying sizes

First Aid Kit

Watering Can — Narrow spout is a must

Brown yard trashbags stand up nicely. Can be recycled

Box Cutter and Blades: Our favorite sharp knife

Ratchet Clippers (For branches)

Knife — Any kitchen knife will do to cut Oasis

Garden Clippers — For branches and thicker stems

Parachute Fabric: Protects surfaces when arranging. Best of all its waterproof.

More Supplies

The Basics — Containers

Urns / Craters / Compotes

Start building a collection of urns, craters and footed compotes.

- Faux cement for large receptions.
- Brass Tall Pedestal for receptions
- Small cement one Smaller altars or receptions
- Black Classic shaped urn
- Green Ceramic Complements soft pastels and fall flowers
- Black with Gold Main Altar Crater. Made of heavy metal
- Black Low Compote Our most used
- Small Urn Small altars or receptions

Boxes

Black and white ceramic boxes are the main containers that we use. The small one holds one block of Oasis. The large holds 1 1/2 blocks. Brass: classic shape for small altars.

Liners

Protect containers and reduce the amount of Oasis needed
We use these liners to go inside many of our containers

Plastic Liner   Paper Mache   White Paper Mache   Sage Green Paper Mache with tar bottom

Clear Lomey dishes sit on top of many urns.

Terracotta Plastic to fit inside urn.

The wilderness and the dry land shall be glad,
  the desert shall rejoice and blossom;
like the crocus it shall blossom abundantly,
  and rejoice with joy and singing.
The glory of Lebanon shall be given to it,
  the majesty of Carmel and Sharon.
They shall see the glory of the Lord,

Isaiah 35:1-2 (NRSV)

The Basics

Your Church Garden

Garden materials can be a very important part of church flower designs. Greenery and flowers from the church garden add that special touch to every arrangement. The branches and stems grown in the gardens are often materials we cannot get at a wholesaler or are too expensive for a church budget.

Garden grown materials are not uniform adding character and a grace to designs. They often have curvilinear shapes which are hard to find elsewhere. Sometimes I go into our garden and find just a few pieces of materials that make the final difference in a design. Much of the greenery that we use from the garden often lasts for weeks.
 It can be cut and reused in a variety of sizes and forms. And, finally, garden materials are budget friendly. In fact, entire arrangements can be made from your church garden.

We have included two "From the Garden" designs in this book.

We concentrate elements of our gardens on greenery that we can use in our arrangements. We also have some flowering plants such as Hydrangea, Abelia, Camellia and Lenten Rose. We try to plant drought tolerant, easy-to-care for shrubs. We have developed a wish list of shrubbery that we want planted. Our grounds team tries to incorporate these materials into their new plantings. Some plants which need space to grow such as Elaeagnus are set in areas where they can grow wild.

Developing a garden for your church can provide you with garden materials for years to come. Learn what grows well in your region. Test out materials and see how they work in designs and arrangements.

Take a walk around your church garden and find spots for these plants. When doing programs at other churches, we often find materials on the grounds that we can use in our designs.

Memorial gifts can be given to create different small gardens around your church. What a wonderful way to commemorate a loved one with a gift that keeps giving as the seasons pass. We have a small garden built by an eagle scout whose parents are no longer living. It is filled with Holly Fern, Sasanqua, Hosta and Lenten Rose that we use all the time. We have been building the Cathedral's gardens for almost twenty years. Little by little your garden will grow.

Encourage your Flower Guild members to bring materials from their gardens as well. We greatly appreciate donations from our Flower Guild members who often bring beautiful cuttings from their gardens. It is truly a glorious site to see their offerings of branches of Sasanqua, Camellia, Nandina, Ligustrum, Elaeagnus, Magnolia and many other specialties.

Here is a walk around the Cathedral's gardens highlighting the materials we use regularly.

Peachtree Entrance to the Cathedral. Gardens with limelight Hydrangea and Abelia

A hidden garden tucked down a hill planted with herbs and perennials

Best Garden Plants for Cut Flower Arrangements

These plants are ideal for a church garden. They grow well in the southern United States. This list has been prepared according to color, function and blooms. Add your own local favorites!

- **Yellow Green**: Aucuba, Variegated Boxwood, Variegated Euonymous

- **Sage/Grey**: Elaeagnus, Stachys (Lamb's Ear), Dusty Miller

- **Dark Green**: Camellia, Dwarf Yedda Hawthorne, Sasanqua, Ligustrum, Cleyera, Osmanthus Fragrans (Tea Olive), Aspidistra (Cast Iron Plant), Magnolia (small leaf varieties)

- **Bright Green**: Pittosporum, Fatsia, Holly Fern, Leucothoe, Helleborus leaves, Boxwood

- **Variegated**: Variegated Pittosporum, Hosta, Daphne, Arum, Variegated Ivy, Variegated Aspidistra

- **Berries**: Nandina, Ligustrum (Blue), Ilex (Holly), leafless Ilex

- **Pretty Drape**: Holly Fern, Leucothoe, Aspidistra, Elaeagnus, Rosemary, Variegated Ivy

- **Line Greens**: Rosemary, Ligustrum, Myrtle, Sasanqua

- **Flowering Shrubs**: Helleborus orientalis (Lenten Rose), Abellia, Cherry, Forsythia, Quince, Hydrangea, especially the varieties: Nikko Blue, Annabelle, Endless Summer, LimeLight and Lacecap varieties

- **Branches**: Curly Willow, Fan Tail Willow, Harry Lauder Walking Sticks

My favorite greenery

Limelight Hydrangea
Late summer blooms from cream to dusty pink, hardy and dries well for fall use.

Rose Creek Abelia
Summer and fall white and Dusty Rose filler.

Variegated Pittosporum
A favorite. Hardy and adds light.

Sasanqua
Late fall early winter blooms. Long graceful branches.

Daphne
Glossy variegated with fragrant winter blooms.

Pittosporum
Base of many arrangements.

Holly Fern
Graceful and dramatic curves for drape.

Basic techniques The Support Structure

Two of the first decisions that need to be made before beginning a design are:
(1) what is your water source and
(2) how you will support your flowers in the arrangement.
Everyone has had the experience of placing flowers in a vase only to have them fall over. Floral foam, most commonly called by its brand name "Oasis", is the arranging structure most often used by church flower arrangers. Oasis allows arrangers to insert flowers in a design and have them stay in position. Flowers can be easily moved to get the best placement possible. And, Oasis supplies a water source to the blooms.

You might choose another technique if your container cannot hold Oasis or If you want the flowers to be placed directly in water. A natural structure using greenery or Hydrangea can be used to create a web structure to support the stems (See Sunflower Example). Chicken wire can also be used to support the stems. A word of caution is that chicken wire is difficult to work with for beginning arrangers.

Oasis

There are two kinds of Oasis. One is "Wet Foam" which is meant for fresh flowers. The other is a dry foam that is designed for silk or dry flowers. We will use the wet foam version in this book.

Techniques for Use

1 **Soak Oasis:** Fill a sink or large plastic tub with enough water to cover Oasis. Place Oasis in water. Let it absorb water on its own.

Tips
Do not run water over Oasis.
Do not press or force down.
Do not cram too many pieces of Oasis in a sink.
Oasis needs room to absorb water.

2 **Cut Oasis:** Oasis can be cut dry or wet. Cut it dry if using at a later date. If using right away, cut it wet. Cut Oasis to fit your container or liner. We most often use liners that fit our containers so we do not have to use too much Oasis, to prevent leaking and to protect the container. You may need one larger piece of Oasis and two on each side to fill the container.

Tip
Leave gaps around Oasis to hold water.

3 **Secure Oasis:** Taping Oasis is generally sufficient in a church setting. Oasis is taped onto dish or container with waterproof tape.

Tip
Waterproof tape sticks best to itself not the container
Set tape off center so there is room to place the center stems
¼" tape is fine for most uses. Use ½" tape for a large piece of Oasis.
Do not tape around front side if not needed
Pinch exposed tape together to tighten hold

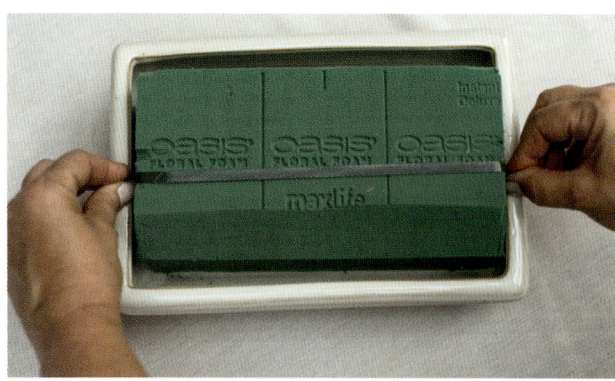

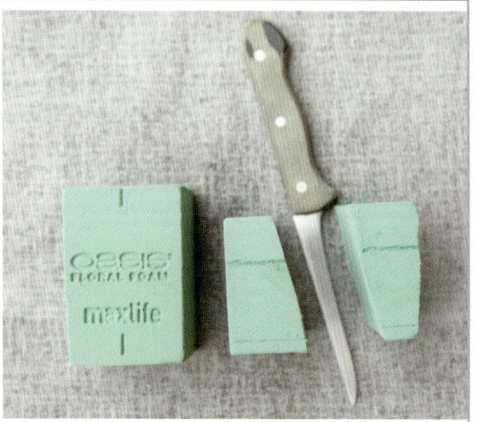

4. **Cover Oasis with Chicken Wire:** If you are using large branches, thick stems or lots of stems, you should cover the Oasis with chicken wire. Also, if a large arrangement will be moved, chicken wire will keep it intact and keep the branches from moving extensively. Cut a chicken wire cap to fit over the Oasis. Using waterproof tape, tape over two sections of holes and run under dish. Secure on opposite side taping over two sections. Place another piece of tape on opposite side.

Tip Save chicken wire caps and reuse.

5. **Watering Oasis:** Oasis absorbs most of its water in the first 24 hours. We find it best to water after the arrangement is covered in its basic greenery. Add more water the next day. After that we find that watering every other day is sufficient.

Tip
Oasis should not be reused for designing. It can harbor bacteria and after a while the holes make it unstable. If you soak too much Oasis, wrap in plastic and store in the refrigerator.

Chicken Wire

Chicken wire has made a comeback in recent years because it allows for a looser style of design that is placed in water. Graceful designs using branch and other garden materials can be accomplished using chicken wire. Since flowers survive best in direct water, they will have a longer life with this technique. A word of caution is that this technique is best for advanced arrangers. It is difficult to move branches once they are in chicken wire.

Techniques for Use

1. Measure diameter of container to be used.
2. Cut piece of chicken wire double the diameter plus 1".
3. Fold wire over and secure with bind wire or green Chenille.
4. Make into a pillow shape.
5. Insert in container and secure with tape to side. Tape all the way around container.
6. Pour in water and begin arranging.
7. Be careful to remove leaves which will be underwater.

Holly Heider Chapple Pillow by Syndicate Sales

Chicken Wire

Holly Heider Chapple Pillow

This new mechanic fits on top of a variety of containers. It comes in diameters of 4", 6", 8" and 10 ½". The pillows fit a variety of containers both low and tall. The pillows enable flower stems to be put directly in water allowing for a longer life.

Techniques for Use

1. Assemble, putting two sides together.
2. Insert greenery in three opposite pieces crossing stems in water.
3. Fill base with greenery crossing stems to hold all in place and to create desired shape.
4. Insert flowers.

Natural structure

Either greenery or Hydrangea can create a web to hold your flowers. The right type of container makes a huge difference with this technique. Containers with a cinched section hold flowers nicely. A classic tapered container also works.

Techniques for Use

1. Fill container with water about 2/3rds up.
2. Add greenery or Hydrangea to create a web inside the vase Strong greenery with a forked branch system works best. (Examples: Salal leaves, Pittosporum, Sasanqua, Aucuba).
3. Insert flowers.
(See "Sundays": Sunflowers vase)

Basic techniques Wiring and More

Wire is produced in a variety of gauges.
The larger the number of the gauge;
the thinner the wire.
Wire comes in boxes of straight pieces and on spools. For wiring individual flowers, straight wire works best. Spool wire is used for wreaths and garlands.

Boxes of wire are generally pretty large so it is best to buy the right size. We typically use 18 gauge for most flowers, particularly for Gerbera Daisies and Roses. Wood picks with wires are also useful for inserting large stems or soft stemmed flowers.

When to wire?

1. Gerbera Daisies which will remain on long stems in Oasis.
2. Roses that will have long stems high in an arrangement.
3. Soft stems such as Calla Lilies, Amaryllis and Tulips.
4. To insert fruit or vegetables into an arrangement.
5. To extend the height of dried material in an arrangement.
6. To extend the length of flowers that will survive out of water .
   (i.e. Cymbidium Orchids, late season Hydrangea)

When not to wire?

1. Only wire if you absolutely need to because it could damage the flowers.
2. Broken stems can generally not be repaired by wiring them. If they break use them lower in the arrangement.
3. Very soft stemmed flowers .

How to wire?

Techniques for commonly wired church flowers

Gerber Technique:
Cut 18 gauge wire in half.
Insert into center of bloom.
Turn top of wire down like a shepherd's hook.
Pull down and gently wrap around the stem.

Fruit and Vegetables:
Depending on where you want the item placed, you can use either a wooden pick or wires attached to a wooden pick. Insert #16 wire through fruit at bottom. Insert second wire on the opposite side making a cross pattern. Attach wire to wooden skewer. Wrap both together with corsage tape. Alternatively insert a long wooden skewer cut to a point into the piece of fruit or vegetable. The green wooden picks expand as they become moist filling the holes as they widen over time.

  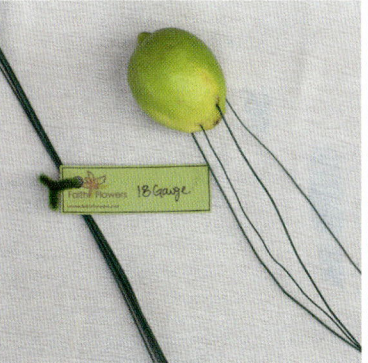 

Rose Technique:
Cut 18 gauge wire in half.
Insert into calyx below the bloom about one half inch.
Gently wrap wire around stem.

Soft Stem Technique: (Callas, Amaryllis and Tulips)
Put wooden pick or garden stake on two sides of the stem about 2-3" from the bottom. Wrap around stem and wood pieces with ¼" waterproof tape. Insert wood pieces into Oasis. Bottom of stem should touch the Oasis. The stem does not need to go into the Oasis or it will tear the Oasis up and damage the stem.

Calla Lilies and Dried Material:
Put a wooden pick on one side of the stem about 2" from bottom. Wrap pick wire around top of stem. Pull down between stem and pick. Wrap around bottom of stem and pick. If the Calla Lily stem is large, you will need to use tape to wrap the top and bottom.

Cymbidium Orchids:
This variety comes on stems with 10 to 12 blooms. It is more economical to break these into single blooms or groups of 2 or 3 blooms. Cut bloom leaving stem attached. Attach pick to stem using wooden pick technique. Wrap with corsage tape to seal in moisture.

Basic design

Classic Triangle

Materials

Classic Triangle Recipe:

Mechanics
Makes one arrangement,
One or two brass boxes (or urns)
Liner if needed
Oasis
Waterproof Tape

Greenery
5-10 Stems Line Greenery
1 Bunch Basic Filler Greenery
1 Bunch Special Greenery (optional)

Flowers
1-2 Bunches Line Flower (1-2 Varieties)
6-12 Stems Focal Flower
5-12 Stems Secondary Flower (optional)
1-2 Bunches Filler
1 Bunch Special (optional)

For larger designs:
Double the quantities

The classic triangle is the basic form of church design. It can be made in a low box or classic urn. Because the shape is clearly defined it shows well in a church. It is pleasingly symmetrical. You will see as you build it out that it is a series of triangles within triangles.
The triangle is often used to represent the Holy Trinity.
The design can be softened by the addition of garden materials. All church flower arrangers should master this design.

Steps

1. Cut Oasis to fit container. Tape one time around.
2. Cover the base with Salal and Leather Leaf.
3. Set the line with the Sasanqua and Larkspur.
   One tall in the center and one at lowest point on each side. Double up center Larkspur to make it fuller.
4. Add a few pieces of greenery at heights in between to transition between the levels.
5. Space the remaining line flowers between them.
6. Place Roses in a triangle pattern.
7. Insert Stock between Roses.

Recipe for Design shown:

Greenery:
Base Greenery: ½ Bunch Leather Leaf
¼ Bunch Salal

Line Greenery: 4 Stems Sasanqua (From the garden)

Flowers:
Line: 8 Stems White Snapdragons
9 Stems Purple Larkspur

Focal: 8 Stems Rose "Early Gray"

Filler: 7 Stems Lilac Stock

Hint
"Color within the lines": Do not let flowers go outside the lines set by the line flowers.

Basic design   Floral Sprays

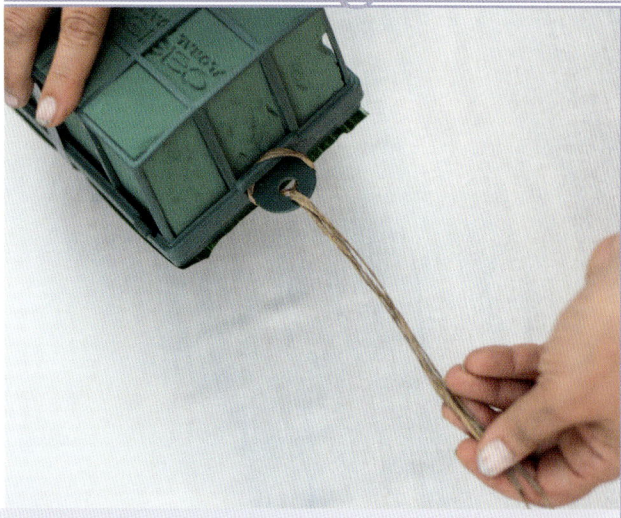

Floral sprays are a beautiful and cost-effective way to decorate a church space. They can be used on pews, columns, doors, the pulpit and more. They unify the look and really fill up the space without using a lot of plant material. For a wedding, they create a take-your-breath-away look. They are also a great way to use garden greenery. Once your team learns the technique, pew sprays are ideal group projects. They can be finished in an assembly line fashion with each person putting in a different kind of material. You can also charge extra for the pew sprays to help build your flower budget. This recipe makes one pew spray. This formula can be used with any color scheme.

Steps You can do steps 1 through 3 ahead of time

1. To secure cage, wrap ¼" tape one time around cage, placing tape on plastic grid.
2. If the back of cages will be seen, the back should be covered. Leaves or a piece of Aspid can be glued on the back.
3. Double a piece of Bind Wire. Insert through both the top of grid and through hole. Leave plenty of wire for hanging.
4. Soak Oasis 5 minutes.
5. Insert one piece of linear material in bottom of cage draping to the desired the length. Use remaining section of greenery at top of cage and/or throughout the body.
6. Place greenery on the cages making a tear drop shape with the bottom being lower than the top. We use the Leather Leaf to make the top, sides and bottom. Lightly cover with Pittosporum leaving gaps for flowers. Garden materials are a nice addition at this point to finish edges and create lush interesting look.
7. Insert line flowers if using. Make one shorter than the other.
8. Place one focal flower at the top in the center. Space remaining ones in zig zag pattern.
9. Place supporting flowers between focal flowers, tucking deeper.
10. Finish with filler flower and greenery. Keep the look light.

Materials

Mechanics
Small Oasis Cage Holder
1/4" Waterproof Tape
Bind Wire
Optional: To be used if covering back of cage: Aspid or leaves
Floral Adhesive

Greenery
½ Bunch Leather Leaf and/or Salal
½ Bunch Pittosporum (Variegated or Green)
1/3 Bunch Interesting or softening greenery (i.e. Italian Variegated Pittosporum, Seeded Eucalyptus, Plumosa)
1 Stem Linear greenery (i.e. Italian Ruscus, Elaeagnus, Leucothoe, Eucalyptus)
Garden material (i.e. Hosta, Gardenia, Camellia)

Flowers Basic recipe. Using line flower is optional. We typically only use it when we are doing draping pew sprays.

Line: (optional)
5 Stems: Snapdragons, Larkspur, Delphinium, Dendobrium Orchids

Focal: 3-6 Stems Roses. Carnations

Supporting: 3-4 Stems Spray Roses, Spray Carnations, Lisianthus,

Filler: 3 Stems Light or textured material (i.e. Waxflower, Baby's Breath, Rice Flower)

Hint
To soften the look, add Plumosa, deflexus or Springereii Fern at the very end.

Basic design Wreaths

Wreaths are an especially appropriate decoration for churches. With their never ending circle, wreaths symbolize eternal life through Jesus Christ, world without end. Evergreen wreaths are almost always used at Christmas. Wreaths create a beautiful entrance for a wedding. They say "Welcome" for most any service or special occasion.

Steps

1. "Chamfer" the edge of the wreath (i.e. cut off hard edge at a slight diagonal all the way around). Wrap ¼" tape all the way around in diagonal about 3" apart. (See photo)
2. Soak Oasis
3. Attach wire and make a good loop to hang.
4. Green Oasis paying particular attention to covering middle section and edges.
5. Leave gaps for flowers.
6. Place Hydrangea in zig zag pattern around wreath.
7. Insert Roses in focal posititions.
8. Cover gaps with Carnations.
9. Add smaller round flowers to fill remaining gaps.
10. Add a touch of filler flowers to soften.

Materials

Mechanics One Oasis wreath form (Oasis form wreaths come in 15" to 24". Remember to add 2" on each side for flowers and greenery. 18" wreath is perfect for a 36" door.)
¼" Waterproof Tape
Heavy covered Wire

Greenery Wreaths use a lot of greenery! For an 18" wreath we used the following
1 Bunch Green Pittosporum
½ Bunch Variegated Pittosporum
½ Bunch Interesting Greenery
 (i.e. Variegated Italian Pittosporum or Seeded Eucalyptus)

Flowers For one Classic Hydrangea and Rose wreath
15 Stems Hydrangea
 (can be mixed colors)
12 Stems Roses
12 Stems Carnations
10 Stems smaller flower (Mums, Spray Carnations, Spray Roses, Freesia)
½ Bunch Filler
 (Waxflower, Baby's Breath, Limonium)

Hint 1
Garden greenery makes a nice addition.

Hint 2
Be sure to place flowers in varying depths: "In and Out"

Basic design

Garland

Garlands are bands of greenery, flowers or both. In Ancient Rome, garlands were used to decorate homes and temples. Plaster garlands adorn columns and ceilings. On mantels you will find garlands in medieval and renaissance paintings draped around statues of Mary or saints. For church decorations, garlands can be used to frame focal elements. They can be used to frame doorways. They can be draped in swags in front of railings or other decorative elements.

Fresh greenery garlands can be ordered premade in a combination of materials. A soft looking garland can be made of Ferns such as Plumosa and Springereii. A heavier garland can include a variety of greenery including Salal leaves, Pittosporum, Italian Ruscus and Ruscus. A beautiful Sage Green and grey color can be achieved by using a variety of Eucalyptus including Seeded Eucalyptus, moon Eucalyptus, Gunni Eucalyptus and more. They can also be made by hand but this can take a lot of time.

At Christmas's garlands incorporating different kinds of Fir are often used around entrances. We use it to decorate our reredos and balcony. Premade Christmas garland is always a quick way to dress up any space. Christmas garland comes in two thicknesses. "Roping", which is thinner, is perfect for around doorways.
Garland is fuller and appropriate for spaces that need a heavy treatment. As a cost savings measure and because we order a lot, we typically use mixed Noble Fir roping. Pre-order in October to get the best price.

Floral garlands can be made by using a pre-made garland tucking in flowers that survive out of water and putting more delicate ones in tubes. A more lush garland filled with flowers can be created using chicken wire and Oasis. We use this type of garland for weddings and major festivals such as Easter and Christmas.

Quick Floral Garlands

Materials
Mechanics
Pre-Made Garland of desired length
Green Plastic Water Tubes 4"

Flowers
Flowers that will survive for 24-48 hours out of water: Carnations, Spray Carnations, Baby's Breath, Spray Mums, Craspedia, Tulips, Limonium

Full Floral Garlands

We prefer to use this technique for full floral garlands. It gives you a good amount of Oasis to provide a water source for your flowers. The Moss joints make it flexible to create a soft drape and to fit around surface. The chicken wire holds everything together after all the stem insertions have been made. It also gives a very nice full floral look.

Steps

1. Cut chicken wire to fit desired length. Wrap chicken wire around Oasis and cut off excess width.
2. Cut Oasis in thirds and place length wise on chicken wire.
3. Insert sections of Mood Moss between Oasis to create a flexible join.
4. Fasten chicken wire around Oasis with zip ties or Chenille wire.
5. Cover back of garland with heavy black plastic bags folded in half to protect surface.
6. Attach heavy wire or zip ties on each end for hanging.
7. Soak Oasis if you have not done so already.
8. Hang the garland.
9. Green Oasis.
10. Insert focal flowers.
11. Fill gaps with smaller flowers.

Materials
Mechanics
One length of chicken wire to fit space being decorated
Oasis bricks cut in 1/3 pieces
Heavy wire
Zip ties - Chenilles
Sheet Moss (can be old and brown)
Moss Pins
Heavy Black Plastic Contractor Bags

Hint
Steps 1 to 6 can be done in advance if Oasis is left dry.

41

Basic Design

Moss Crosses

Moss crosses placed on doors greet parishioners on many occasions including Easter and weddings.
On regular Sundays they can be used with leftover bits and pieces. The forms can be reused if kept in a cool dark place. Only the Iglu needs to be replaced.

Steps

1. Double bind wire and thread through Iglu. Make sure to get the wire through the cage grid and the plastic with the hole.
2. Use doubled bindwire to make loop for hanging cross OR hang with metal "S" hook attached to hole on back.
3. Attach Moss to cross using greening pins. If Moss is slightly damp it will stretch better. (NOTE: Do not soak cross)
4. Slice off top of Iglu form to first row of grid. Soak Oasis Iglu and attach to cross.
5. Place greenery on the iglu to cover lightly leaving gaps for flowers. Garden materials are a nice addition at this point.
6. Insert line flowers following the line of the cross.
7. Insert focal flowers in a triangle shape.
8. Place supporting flowers between focal flowers, tucking deeper.
9. Finish with filler flower and interesting greenery. Keep the look light.

Materials

Mechanics
Oasis cross wreath form
1/4" Waterproof Tape
Bind Wire to hang
1/3 Box Sheet Moss
2-3 Greening Pins
Iglu Holder (Smaller size)

Greenery
Bits of greenery to cover Oasis cage. Pittosporum paired with interesting greenery such as Italian Variegated Pittosporum, Variegated Boxwood and Seeded Eucalyptus adds texture and light.

Flowers
Basic recipe.
Using line flower is optional.
We typically use it when we want a dramatic effect.

Line: 4 Stems Snapdragons, Larkspur, Delphinium, Calcynia

Focal: 3 Stems Roses. Large Mums, Easter Lilies

Supporting: 3-4 Stems Spray Roses, Spray Carnations, Lisianthus,

Filler: 3 Stems Light material such as Waxflower or Baby's Breath

Hint
To revive old Moss, soak in very hot water for 30 minutes. Squeeze and use.

Basic design Topiaries

Once the base is made, you can reuse these topiaries over and over again. We have done them at Christmas with Holly, Fir and Berries. They are great entrance pieces for special events. This technique can also be used for table top topiaries using small cages. They do need a lot of greenery, but a variety of greens can be used. They don't require a lot of flowers either!

Steps

1. Drill holes in back of 3 cages .
2. Attach cage with screws into the pole.
3. Make concrete according to directions on container. Pour into plastic liner. Leave a two inch gap between top of concrete and pot so there is room for top dressing of Moss.
4. Insert pole and hold in place until concrete sets. Let cure as long as needed.
5. Insert wet Oasis and cover with cage top .
6. Wrap around all cages with floral tape.
7. Cover densely with greenery to create a round shape.
8. Insert flowers.
9. Finish base with Mood Moss.

Materials

Mechanics
1 Decorative Pot for base
   (heavy ceramic or clay pot)
Plastic Pot that fits inside decorative pot
Quick drying cement
Birch pole (about 3" in diameter
   and 6 to 8' tall)
3 Large Cages
Green Floral Tape
Drill
Screws

Greenery
2 Bunches Green Pittosporum
1 Bunch Variegated Pittosporum
1 Bunch Leather leaf
4 Stems Aucuba
Mood Moss

Flowers
8 Stems Lavender Daisy Mums
6 Stems Peach Spray Carnations

Hint
Do Ahead: Can be greened 2 or 3 days in advance.

And God said, "Let the waters under the sky be gathered together into one place, and let the dry land appear." And it was so. God called the dry land Earth, and the waters that were gathered together he called Seas. And God saw that it was good.
Then God said, "Let the earth put forth vegetation: plants yielding seed, and fruit trees of every kind on earth that bear fruit with the seed in it." And it was so. The earth brought forth vegetation: plants yielding seed of every kind, and trees of every kind bearing fruit with the seed in it. And God saw that it was good.

Gen. 1:9-12 NRSV

Sunday flowers Introduction

Flowers in churches enhance the worship experience for everyone. Their beauty and color adorn and accent the design of the worship space.
Flowers and greenery bring an element of nature inside reflecting God's glorious creation.
Their seasonality marks the church calendar as the seasons pass. Their scent, and the memories they evoke, move worshippers in countless ways. Every Sunday someone tells us that the flowers were beautiful or moving to them.
As the music, liturgy, architecture and flowers all come together, the community celebrates. Flowers are an important liturgical art form. Flower arrangements are to the service of God, clergy and the parishioners.

Sunday — A Grand Classic Triangle

The classic triangle is the basic shape of church flower arranging. Because of its strong shape, triangle designs are easily seen in large church spaces where flowers are often placed far from the viewer. The shape is pleasing to look at. The triangle may also represent the holy trinity.

Steps

These steps can be followed to create a classic triangle shape. The Flowers used in the design are put in parentheses.

1. Soak and cut Oasis to fit liner. Oasis should be about 4" above edge of container.
2. Chamfer edges: Cut off sharp corners and edges to make the beginning of a rounded shape.
3. Optional: Cover with chicken wire cap. Tape in place. Use chicken wire if there are a lot of large stems or if arrangement will be transported. (See Structure Techniques)
4. Cover base loosely with greenery.
5. Water Oasis at this point (Becomes hard to do later).
6. Set Line (Snapdragons and Tuberose).
   a. Start with three tallest pieces of greenery. Place in the center and one on each side. Stay close to the center stem.
   b. Place greenery on lowest point on each side creating your triangle.
   c. Follow with line flowers (Larkspur, Snapdragons, etc.)
   d. Fill in between top and bottom stems with line greenery. Stagger placement slightly to create depth and softness.
7. Insert Leather Leaf in middle and edges to cover stems lightly.
8. Place Focal Flowers (Roses).
   a. Start at top slightly below center line flower.
   b. Place #2 and #3 below in triangle pattern.
   c. Place another one in just below repeating pattern until a large triangle is created. This step will take 8 to 12 flowers depending upon the size.
9. Place secondary flowers (Carnations) in between focal flowers. Tuck deeper than focal flower. Let some cascade downward.
10. Insert some of the Seeded Eucalyptus in middle and sides.
11. Insert filler.
    a. Light filler towards middle (Orlaya).
    b. Cascading filler around edges and touches in middle (Calcynia).
    c. Other special flowers should be added if they emphasize the line (Spray Roses).

Materials

Mechanics
- Urn 20 to 24" Height (Well weighted on the bottom)
- Liner to fit
- Chicken Wire
- Floral Tape

Greenery
- 6 Stems Eucalyptus parviflora
- 6 Stems Camellia branches
- 1 Bunch Leather Leaf
- 1 Bunch Pittosporum
- 1 Bunch Seeded Eucalyptus

Flowers
- Line: 8 Stems Snapdragons, 8 Stems Larkspur, 8 Stems Tuberose
- Focal: 12 Stems Rose "Caramel"
- Secondary: 12 Stems Carnation "Merlot Crimson"
- Filler: 1 Bunch Orlaya, 1 Bunch Peach Stock
- Special: 1 Bunch Calcynia

Hint 1
Emphasize the lower area to create a soft and dramatic skirt. It will make the line look longer and more elegant. Use extra soft draping materials such as Calcynia or soft greenery.

Hint 2
Save about half of the Seeded Eucalyptus or special greenery to put in the front so it can be seen and does not become buried in the arrangement.

Sunday Classic Triangle with Hydrangea

Using readily available Hydrangea, this version of the classic triangle is a simple, affordable design. Heavier flowers such as Gladiolas and Lilies pair best with Hydrangea. Monte Casino add a touch of lightness.

Steps

1. Cover the base of the box with Pittosporum and Salal.
2. Add a few pieces of greenery at heights in between to transition between the levels.
3. Set the line with the Gladiolas placing one in the center and one on each side of the lowest point.
4. Place the remaining Gladiolas evenly between the top and bottom. Set them in and out slightly for depth.
5. Insert Hydrangea in triangle shape alternating varieties.
6. Place the Lilies in between starting at the top.
7. Trim Monte Casino into a slimmer grouping of blooms. Place between Lilies.
8. Use bits of Monte Casino throughout the design.

Materials

Mechanics
Makes one arrangement.
Double for a pair.
One box or urn
Liner if needed
Waterproof Tape

Greenery
¼ Bunch Salal
½ Bunch Variegated Pittioporum
½ Bunch Leather Leaf

Flowers
Line: 9 Stems Yellow Gladiolas

Focal: 6 Stems Yellow Asiatic Lilies

Secondary: 6 Stems Blue Hydrangea

Filler: 5 Stems Monte Casino

Hint
Color within the lines: Do not let flowers go outside the lines set by the line flowers.

Sunday
Classic Triangle Two Ways

If the basic triangle is made in two boxes, the design can be used to create two different shapes by splitting and rearranging the boxes. This design nicely frames the cross as the flowers descend towards its base.

Steps

1. Set Oasis in two identical boxes.
2. Follow instructions for Classic Triangle.
3. Split boxes in two descending down toward the base of the cross.
4. Add one Snapdragon to the outer side to make the height of both sides match.

Materials

Mechanics
Two low boxes
Liner if needed
Waterproof tape

Greenery
Base:
½ Bunch Pittosporum
¼ Bunch Salal

Flowers
Line: 9-10 Stems Snapdragons

Focal: 8 Stems "Cool Water" Rose

Secondary: 3 Stems White "Artic" Spray Mum

Filler: 4 Stems White Spray Carnations
½ Bunch Bupleurum

Sunday Monochromatic

Monochromatic designs are very effective in church spaces. Using flowers of one color really makes a strong impact.
This color scheme works well in a church space where flowers are often set very far back. Try all yellow, all green, all orange, or all lavender. There will be subtle changes in tone that add nice contrast and depth. You can see the texture contrasts here of the different materials.
This is my go to plan when I am designing.

Steps

1. Set up mechanics .
2. Cover the base with dark green Pittosporum.
3. Set the upper line with the green Gladiolas.
4. Counter balance with Bells of Ireland descending at an angle.
5. Use the foxtail foliage and Wegelia to transition the between the two elements.
6. Add a few pieces of Foxtail and Bells to the left side to soften.
7. Accent the focal area with Spider and Button Mums.
8. Group Seeded Eucalyptus in sections to create textural differences and impact.
9. Add persimmons last so that they show. Place in focal area and draping down.

Materials

Mechanics
Urn
Plastic Liner
1 Oasis (Medium Size) and ½ Regular Brick

All Green

Line: 5 Stems Green Gladiolas
7 Stems Bells of Ireland
6 Stems Foxtail Foliage "Merereii"

Focal: 10 Stems "Green Tea" Rose
4 Stems Hosta

Filler: 1 Bunch Leafless Seeded Eucalyptus
5 Stems Green Spider Mums
3 Stems Green Button Mums "Yoko Ono"
2 Stems Variegated Pittosporum
3 Stems Dwarf Yedda Hawthorne

Special: 5 Stems Green Persimmon Branches
5 Stems Poppy Pods

Greenery: 3 Stems Weigela Foliage
1 Bunch Green Pittosporum

Hint
Grouping flowers really helps to make the types of flowers used stand out and to create the line

Sunday

Caroline's Cascade

This design is one of the favorites of a long time Flower Guild member. It has a swoop of strong colored flowers cascading through the arrangement. Typically the color palette is limited to two colors. It is very effective in a large space.

Steps

1. Cover the base with greenery.
2. Group Holly Fern on sides for drape.
3. Set the line with the tall greenery and Trachelium.
4. Insert the tallest Rose slightly to the right of center.
5. Insert the remaining Roses in a curvilinear line cascading through the design to the opposite corner.
6. Fill in the right side with Heather grouping it together.
7. Group Waxflower, Button Mums and Hypericum to fill out each side.

Materials

Mechanics
One Crater with liner
Oasis

Greenery
Pittosporum
Magnolia
Holly Fern
Tea Olive

Flowers
Line: ½ Bunch Green Trachelium
Focal: 20 Stems Rose "Deep Purple"
Filler: ½ Bunch Lavender Heather
10 Stems Green Hypericum Berries
7 Stems Green Button Mums
½ Bunch Purple Waxflowers

Sunday

Mary and Martha

The key to this design is that one side is larger and one smaller than the other reflecting the story of Mary and Martha.

[38] Now as they went on their way, he entered a certain village, where a woman named Martha welcomed him into her home. [39] She had a sister named Mary, who sat at the Lord's feet and listened to what he was saying. [40] But Martha was distracted by her many tasks; so she came to him and asked, "Lord, do you not care that my sister has left me to do all the work by myself? Tell her then to help me." [41] But the Lord answered her, "Martha, Martha, you are worried and distracted by many things; [42] there is need of only one thing. (a) Mary has chosen the better part, which will not be taken away from her."
Luke 10:30-42 NRSV

Steps

1. Cover the base with greenery.
2. Set the line with Eremurus making one side significantly taller than the other.
3. Insert the curly Willow and wrap around and in between the Eremurus.
4. Place the Roses, grouping them together. Use a smaller amount on the smaller side.
5. Place the Gerber Daisies in the lower sections angling the boxes toward each other.
6. Fill in with taller pieces of Cypress and treated fall leaves.
7. Fill in with Carnations continuing the pattern of Roses and Gerbers.
8. Group Hypericum to create texture in the base.
9. Use Millet to emphasize the line and add contrast.

Materials

Mechanics
2 Ceramic Boxes
Oasis

Greenery
Variegated Pittosporum
Nandina
Cypress
Treated fall leaves

Flowers
5 Stems Yellow Eremurus ("Foxtail Lily")
12 Stems Rose "High and Happy"
7 Stems Orange-Red Gerber Daisies
10 Stems Orange Carnations "Hermes"
10 Stems Orange Yellow Hypericum
5 Stems Burgundy Spray Mums
1/2 Bunch Coral Curly Willow
1 Bunch Millet

Sunday Golden Garden Greenery

Straight from the garden comes a yellow color palette achieved by using yellow toned greenery contrasted by dark materials.
A touch of Nandina adds a bit of sparkle to the design.

Steps

1. Set Oasis in dish and tape. Soak Oasis.
2. Set line with Camellia branches emphasizing triangle shape here.
3. Create focal area with Euonymus.
4. Fill with Aucuba.
5. Add touches of Nandina.

Materials

Mechanics
Plastic Dish
Regular brick Oasis

Garden Materials
5 Stems Golden Euonymus
8 Stems Camellia
6 Stems Pittosporum
6 Stems Aucuba Japonica Gold Dust
6 Stems Nandina

Sunday From the Garden

Using greenery and materials from your church garden is a great way to keep the budget down. Use all greenery on a Sunday when there are no memorial donations. All of the materials in this arrangement were from the church, my home garden and my studio. Take a look at the reference sheet on plants that would be good to plant on the church grounds. Planting now will pay off in years to come. We do not bother planting flowers which require more maintenance, except Hydrangea which is pretty care free in our area.

When planning greenery you should think about it just as you would a regular design. You will need greenery for line and drape. You will need a focal element and supporting stems. And finally add filler materials. In terms of color it is best to have a theme to unite the arrangement. In the first example, we have used dark and light green and dusty greys. The second example uses greenery with yellows.

Steps

1. Set Oasis in container and cover with chicken wire. (chicken wire is often helpful with greenery arrangements because of the size of the stems.). Chamfer edges to make dome shape.
2. Cover boxes with basic greenery. (Pittosporum)
3. Use the Magnolia to set a curving line through the middle of the arrangement draping down over the edge of the compote.
4. Insert the Elaeagnus to emphasize and extend the line of the Magnolia and soften the design.
5. Group the Daphne with its distinctive variegated edge as an accent.
6. Use the Dusty Miller to create the focal area.
7. Insert the Limelight Hydrangea following the lines.
8. Fill shape out with Dwarf Yedda Hawthorne, placing it loosely.

Materials

Mechanics
Compote style container
Plastic Liner
Medium Oasis
2 Halves of bricks

All Green

Line: 7 Stems Elaeagnus
5 Stems Magnolia

Focal: 4 Stems Dusty Miller
9 Stems Limelight Hydrangea (small heads)

Filler: 4 Stems Dark Green Pittosporum
2 Stems Variegated Pittosporum
3 Stems Dwarf Yedda Hawthorne

Special: 3 Stems Daphne

Hint
Let the shape of the greenery dictate the shape of the arrangement.

Sunday Moongate

One of our favorite designs.
We love the way the greenery gently encircles the cross.

Steps

1. Cover boxes with greenery. Place greenery in radial method as if springing from the center points on each side.
2. Press Italian Ruscus gently between your thumb and fingers to bend it into a curvilinear shape.
3. Insert Ruscus into Oasis at back corners and circle the cross. Use a small piece of green wire to secure pieces to each other. Add a lighter piece over the center to thicken.
4. Place one piece of Ruscus on the outer side of each box gently descending downward.
5. Set the line with Larkspur radiating from center.
6. Place the Snapdragons as if they are growing in the center letting their curves take a natural shape.
7. Place your focal flowers towards the center of each box lightly covering the base of the cross.
8. Add a touch of Waxflower to lighten edges.
9. Use wisps from Larkspur towards the front.

Materials

Mechanics
2 Ceramic Boxes or Green Plastic Dishes
2 Oasis Bricks
1 Cross
Green Bind Wire

Greenery
5 Stems Italian Ruscus
 (or curving plant materials)
½ Bunch Green Pittosporum
½ Bunch Variegated Pittisproum
4 Stems Variegated Boxwood
½ Bunch Leather Leaf

Flowers
Line: 8 Stems White Larkspur
 6 Stems Pink Larkspur
 8 Stems Appleblossom Snaps

Focal: 4 Stems Stargazer Lily
 8 Stems "Snowy Jewel" Rose

Filler: ¼ Bunch Waxflower

> **Hint**
> Radial placement of material is very important to achieve this effect.

Sunday   Summer Sunflowers

During the summer Sunflowers are plentiful and well-priced. The problem is what to do with them. Their heads are so heavy that they droop. Here are a couple of quick ideas.

Sunflower Wreath

Brighten the entrance to your church with this cheerful wreath. You can use leftover Sunflowers to make it. Makes one 15" Wreath

Steps

See Basic Wreath Technique Steps 1 to 3.
1. When placing flowers start with larger flowers and spread evenly on wreath.
2. Remove petals of any Sunflowers where petals are not in good condition. Place evenly on wreath.
3. Fill gaps with Viking Mums.
4. Finish by inserting Ivy strands and winding through design.
5. Add a contrasting bow.

Sunflowers in a vase

Sunflowers and Pittosporum are the base. We added some Delphinium, Phlox and Kangaroo Paw to make it more interesting.

Steps

1. Fill vase tightly with Pittosporum to create a web and branch system to support Sunflowers.
2. Add Sunflowers in varying heights.
3. Add materials to lighten the look: We used Delpinium, Phlox, and Kangaroo Paw.

Hint
We find that using a mix of varieties and sizes is the best way to avoid them looking like eyes on the altar.

Materials **Mechanics**
15" Wreath Form

Greenery
½ Bunch Variegated Pittosporum
½ Bunch Green Pittosporum
5 Pieces Variegated Ivy

Flowers
Any combination of sunflowers will work. You need 10 to 15 total
5 Stems "Sunbright" Sunflowers Large
5 Stems "Sunbeam" Sunflowers
12 Stems "Sunbright" Sunflowers Small
4 Stems "Viking" Mums

Materials **Mechanics**
A heavy vase with a cinched section

Greenery
Pittosporum Regular and Variegated
Florida Ruscus
Other garden greenery such as
  Camellia or Gardenia leaves

Flowers
Any combination of sunflowers
  will work. You need 10 to 15 total
4 Stems "Sunbright" Sunflowers Large
4 Stems "Sunbeam" Sunflowers
7 Stems "Sunbright" Sunflowers Small
6 Stems "Sunsplash" Sunflower
1 Bunch "Skywaltz" Delphinium
½ Bunch Yellow Kangaroo Paw
8 Stems White Phlox

Hint
Remove petals of damaged Sunflowers to create a new flower of the center.

Sunday — Dramatic Summer Garden

This design is perfect for the months when dramatic eremerus and lovely Abellia is in season. This asymmetrical design was inspired by Holly Chapple.
We love the color palette of soft pinks, peaches and cream accented by deep burgundy and hot pink.

Steps

1. Tape and chicken wire Oasis in dish (see Basics Techniques for instructions).
2. Cover base with Pittosporum and Salal.
3. Set the line with the eremerus since it is so distinctive in its shape. Angle one side up and one side down.
4. Use line greenery to reinforce the line. Go with the natural flow of these pieces.
5. Insert Snapdragons to reinforce line.
6. Focal flowers (Roses and Gerrondo Gerbers) in central area of design.
7. Fill gaps in main section with Rose Creek Abellia, Stock and Hydrangea. Continue to follow line.
8. Finish with groupings of Tulips and bits of Abellia to soften the edges.

Materials

Mechanics
Large Footed Style Arrangement
11" Lomey Dish
½" Tape
Chicken Wire
Large Oasis

Greenery
½ Bunch Pittosporum
¼ Bunch Variegated Pittosporum
½ Bunch Salal

From the garden:
6 Stems Draping Standard Abellia
5 Stems "Rose Creek" Abellia
5 Stems Ileagnus

Flowers
Line: 5 Stems Eremerus
8 Stems Burgundy Snapdragons
6 Stems Pink Larkspur
10 Stems Hot Pink Tulips

Focal: 10 Stems Peach "Carpe Diem" Rose
10 Stems Light pink Gerrondo Gerbera "Terra Posh"

Filler: 8 Stems Magenta Stock
4 Stems Hydrangea "Limelight"

Hint 1
Leave line flowers fairly open. Negative space is needed to make effect

Hint 2
Add flowers angling backwards in center section.

Sunday Small Garden Compote

Harkening back to the days of Sheila McQueen and Constance Spry, this style of design is a good one to use when you have bits and pieces from the garden.
It can showcase special delicate flowers such as the Helleborus. It is also a great way to use leftover bits from prior weeks or other arrangements. Its soft draping shape creates that "just picked look". To create a more natural shape, we have used locally grown Hydrangea which has smaller heads and looser shapes. Adding wispy bits of flowers and greenery adds the finishing touch.
This lovely design works best in small chapels or side tables.

Steps

1. Create a chicken wire "pillow". Here's how: Measure diameter of compote. Cut double the amount of chicken wire plus one inch. Cut chicken wire into circle shape. Fold in half. Gently shape into a pillow about 1" thick. Attach edges with bind wire or Chenille.
2. Put floral frog in center of compote. Use green cling to attach.
3. Put clear floral tape around edges of the pillow and anchor to the sides in four places. Tape all the way round the top of the container. Add water.
4. Insert draping bits of greenery.
5. Set line with draping flowers.
6. Insert tall flowers into floral frog.
7. Fill with larger greenery and Hydrangea.
8. Insert special flowers (Helleborus and Cone Flowers) allowing them to drape in their natural direction.
9. Tuck Roses deeper for color.
10. Add loose bits of Tweedia to soften.

Materials

Mechanics
Footed compote style container
Chicken Wire
2" frog
Bind Wire
½" Clear floral tape
Cling

Greenery

Line: 2 Stems Bay Leaf

Filler: 2 Stems Pokeweed (Locally grown)
5 Stems Hosta
3 Stems Dwarf Yedda Hawthorne

Flowers
Line: 6 Stems Blue Tweedia
5 Stems White Campanula

Focal: 5 Stems Helleborus
4 Stems Purple Coneflower (Locally grown)
3 Stems "Mother of Pearl" Rose
3 Stems White Lisianthus

Filler: 6 Stems Antique Blue Hydrangea (Locally grown)

Wispy: 3 Stem Blue Nigella
3 Stems Lavender Scabiosa

Hint 1
Do not forget the drape. The more you can add flowers that drape on the bottom, the softer the shape will be.

Hint 2
Loose wispy bits make this design.

Sunday
Potted Composition

Potted compositions are a good way to create an arrangement which will last for weeks, sometimes months.
We find these are particularly useful in the summer months when volunteers are scarce. They can be made with any types of plants including Orchids.

Steps

1. Line pot or container with heavy black plastic if it might leak.
2. Place a layer of lava rocks on the bottom for drainage.
3. Insert tall plant first.
4. Insert draping plants.
5. Fill with additional plants.
6. Finish with Mood Moss if desired.

Hint
When using Orchids leave them in their pots.

Hint
The key is to make sure all the plant material has similar watering needs. For example, since Orchids need very little water, they should be planted ideally with drought tolerant materials.

Materials

Mechanics
Bowl or plastic lined basket deep enough to hold rocks and the plants
Potting Soil
Lava Rocks or small stone
1-2 Draping plants
1 Tall plant
2 Medium size softer plants such as Ferns

Plants
Aglaonema Silver Bay
Fern Silver Queen
Autumn Fern
Philodendron Xanadu

Sunday Winter Wonderland

This arrangement shows how two pieces can be used to connect and extend a design. This technique creates the illusion of a much larger arrangement. Very little flowers are required. The most important part of the design is the connecting pieces which were branches with faux snow. The design can be created on a column as shown or on an altar connecting to the floor.

Inspired by a recent snow, all materials were chosen to create the essence of snow in a winter forest. White ceramic containers were used to repeat the color and to make coverage easier.

Steps

1. Insert Oasis in container leaving at least two inches above the top containers so there is room for the descending branch and materials.
2. Cover the base of each container with Variegated Pittosporum.
3. Insert bits of Cypress for contrast.
4. Set line with the branches connecting the top and lower sections making an "S" shape.
5. Repeat line with Delphinium.
6. Create a strong focal area in the main container with the contrasting focal elements.
7. Repeat a smaller area on the lower section.
8. Add Queen Anne's Lace and Baby's Breath to soften.

Materials

Mechanics
1 Round White Ceramic Dish
1 White Ceramic Column
Oasis

Greenery
1 Bunch Variegated Pittosporum
5 Stems Leucothoe
3 Stems Tea Olive
6 Stems Cypress

Flowers
Line: 5 Branches with faux snow
5 Stems White Hybrid Delphinium
3 Stems White Kale

Focal: 5 Stems White Spider Mums "White Anastatia"
5 Stems White Disbud Mums "White Zonar"

Filler: 5 Stems Queen Anne's Lace
½ Bunch Baby's Breath

Sunday   Garden Altar

A garden altar is created with flowers placed as if they are growing in a garden. Flowers are grouped together with random ones interspersed as they might spring up in nature. This design is very effective in a number of color combinations. One of my favorites is white and green. It can be placed behind an altar, below an altar or anywhere with a long horizontal span of space.
The design can use as little or as much material as you want.

Steps

1. Set up mechanics using a variety of containers. A deeper dish in the middle allows for stem placement depth.
2. A strong vertical element is needed for this design. The line flowers need to be placed vertically with a slight twist so that they look like they are naturally growing towards the sun. Gladiolas work well as the size of their bloom carries well to the back of a church.
3. Set the areas for taller elements of the design by grouping the Gladiolas and Snapdragons. The center should have one substantial tall grouping. Be careful to balance the tall sections.
4. Place the flowers so that some are leaning out and backwards.
5. Place the next largest and most important blooms, the Amaryllis Insert the Roses using in and out placement of the stems.
6. Use the Salal and Leather Leaf at this point to accent the flowers in the tall area placing between the stems.
7. Insert Spray Roses and Carnations to augment the Roses and add a bit of looseness.
8. Use Berries and Seeded Eucalyptus to finish the lower level and cover any gaps. Group these into clusters.

Materials

Greenery
2 Bunches Pittosporum
1 Bunch Seeded Eucalyptus
1 Bunch Leather Leaf
½ Bunch Salal

Flowers
9 Stems Mauve Gladiolas
10 Stems Snapdragons "Talisman"
5 Stems Amaryllis "Mocca"
10 Stems Rose "Hermosa"
8 Stems Red Rose "Corazon"
6 Stems Rose "Carousel"
8 Stems Burgundy Gerber Daisies
10 Stems Red Tulips
5 Stems Peach Spray Carnations
10 Stems Coral Hypericum
8 Stems Sweet Sara Spray Rose
1 Bunch Spray Leucadendron
1 Bunch Coral Curly Willow

Hint
Leave distinctive areas of high and low. Negative open space makes the design work.

Sunday   Pumpkin Stacks

Materials

Mechanics
4 Long Cream Ceramic Dishes
6 Bricks Regular Oasis

Greenery
Variegated Pittosporum
Salal
Sasanqua
Cleyera

Flowers
9 Pumpkins: variety of colors/texture
4 Small gourds

Line: 9 Stems Orange Gladiolas
9 Stems Bells of Ireland
5 Stems Green Trachelium

Focal Terraced 6 Stems Orange Gerber Daisies
Elements: 10 Stems Orange Rose "Confidential"
9 Stems Green Spider Mums
5 Stems Rust Disbud "Paladon"

Filler: 6 Stems Green Mums "Athos"
10 Stems Peach Hypericum Berries

Terracing flowers by placing them in a stair step pattern is a very effective technique in churches.
A vertical garden is created on an altar with two levels in the colors of Pumpkins. A variety of Pumpkins are stacked upon one another to repeat the terracing of the flowers.

Steps

1 Place Oasis in dishes and tape.
2 Cover base with greenery.
3 Set areas of line flowers and greenery spacing them vertically in three groups.
4 Place Roses in groupings in a stair step fashion with heads pointing upwards.
5 Repeat stair step pattern with other terraced elements.
6 Place filler flowers in lower areas to add texture and brightness.

Hint
Be sure to leave negative space, areas of openness.

Sunday Summer Fun

Visit the wholesaler's cooler and see what is seasonally different. I found these locally grown rusty orange Celosia Plume and orange marigolds. The colors were selected to reflect flowers growing in the heat of late summer staying within a narrow range of yellow to orange to red. Red Celosia and Gomphrena, which had just come in season, added great textural interest. The yellow orange ranunculus made the perfect color transition. Bright green with yellow spotted Aucuba livened up the greenery and tied it into the design.

Steps

1. Set Oasis in liner. Tape. Soak.
2. Cover the base with greenery. Use Aucuba to break up the greenery and set the line.
3. Set the line with Celosia Plume and Millet.
4. Place Marigolds throughout as focal element.
5. Add red elements of Celosia and Viburnum Berries.
6. Add Ranunculus placing in-and-out.
7. Add Gomphrena and Cone Flower centers for a touch of whimsy.

Materials

Mechanics
One medium sized urn
Paper mache liner
Waterproof tape

Greenery
½ Bunch Green Pittosporum
½ Bunch Leather Leaf
4 Stems Aucuba

Flowers
Line: 10 Stems Celosia Plume
10 Stems Foxtail Millet

Focal: 10 Stems Orange Marigolds

Supporting: 5 Stems Celosia Red
8 Stems Orang/Yellow Ranunculus

Filler: ½ Bunch Gomphrena
8 Stems Cone Flower Centers
1 Bunch Yellow Yarrow
5 Stems Hydrangea from the garden
3 Stems Red Viburnum Berry

'Arise, my love, my fair one,
   and come away;
for now the winter is past,
   the rain is over and gone.
The flowers appear on the earth;
   the time of singing has come,
and the voice of the turtle-dove
   is heard in our land.
The fig tree puts forth its figs,
   and the vines are in blossom;
   they give forth fragrance.
Arise, my love, my fair one,
   and come away.

Song of Solomon 2:7-13 (NRSV)

Weddings

Weddings are a celebration of the public commitment of two people to one another. They are joyful occasions. Flowers typically play a prominent role in the beginning of a new life together. The flowers in the church can range from simple garden flowers in a vase to grand arrays of flowers. The design for the church flowers sets the tone for the design of the entire wedding including the bouquets and reception flowers.

Introduction

Wedding flowers at churches can include the altar flowers, pew sprays, wreaths, garlands, pedestals and reception area arrangements. A bright floral wreath on the doors into the church is a welcoming sign for wedding guests. Pew sprays create a beautiful aisle for the ceremony procession. Additional arrangements may also be made for pedestals at the front of the church or in the narthex or reception areas. Some churches have aisle candles that can be used for the ceremony as well.

The flowers for church wedding ceremonies can be created by the Flower Guild or professional florists depending upon the custom of the church and the availability and talents of the Flower Guilds. Flower Guilds should consider arranging flowers for weddings. When Flower Guilds arrange flowers for weddings, it is a lovely coming together of the community to celebrate with the couple and family. Since flower guilds are volunteer based, it may not be possible to do all the flowers so start with the altar flowers. Many churches provide altar flowers only and allow outside florists to bring in the extra flowers such as pew sprays and wreaths. With training your guild members can do everything from wedding altar flowers to pew sprays.

Flower Guilds can charge a reasonable fee for the flowers to cover the cost and help grow their flower budgets. The couple will get beautiful flowers lovingly created at a good price and the Flower Guild can build a budget for things like containers, training and flowers. Finally, flowers are often left on the altar for the Sunday services so they can do double duty. Parishioners enjoy the flowers the next day and celebrate the wedding in the Sunday service.

Weddings

Classic Wedding Urns

A classic wedding flower design for a ceremony

Steps

1. Cut Oasis to fit liner. Should be 3-4" higher than the rim of the liner.
2. Tape all the way around in a "cross" pattern.
3. Cover lightly with Pittosporum.
4. Place straightest Italian Ruscus in center in back of container.
5. Place one Ruscus on each side of the tall one.
6. Place two Ruscus on the lower section of each side to create the basic line of the drape.
7. Place the Snapdragons following the lines of the Ruscus.
8. Fill in the gaps with Larkspur to make one full triangle.
9. Insert Hydrangea in triangle shape.
10. Place Roses in gaps. Be sure to have them protrude further out than Hydrangea.
11. Fill in with Stock.
12. Place Sasanqua and Leucothoe on each side to build out and to emphasize the drape.

Materials

Mechanics
Urn (or a pair of urns)
Plastic Liner
Waterproof Tape
Grande Oasis

Greenery
½ Bunch Green Pittosporum
½ Bunch Variegated Pittosporum
7 Stems Italian Ruscus
½ Bunch Salal

From the garden
4 Branches Sassanqua
4 Branches Leucothoe

Flowers
Line: 7 White Snapdragons
7 White Larkspur

Focal: 7 Vendela Rose
7 White Mondial
Filler:
Filler: 8 White Stock
7 White Hydrangea

Blush Version of the Classic Urn

Weddings

Hydrangea Orb

As a wedding florist, this style is currently one of the most commonly requested. It is a simple design that can be done by Flower Guilds. The flowers can be placed on top of a glass cylinder or any urn. Very little greenery is typically showing. Greenery is used mostly to help keep the moisture in the Oasis.

Steps

1. Place Grande Oasis sideways on Lomey dish.
2. Cut Oasis brick in half diagonally and place on each side of Lomey dish - Add small piece on each side.
3. Tape around Oasis twice.
4. Cover Oasis with greenery.
5. Measure 16" in diameter vertically and horizontally.
6. Place Hydrangea at top and center 16" from bottom.
7. Place one on each side in middle 16" apart.
8. Place on front and back bottom to make a quadrant
9. Start filling in with Hydrangea. Keep round shape. Widest in the middle points and top. Tapers inward at other points.
10. Fill gaps with Carnations.
11. Spread Roses evenly around Hydrangea.

Hint 1
A mix of light blue or pink and white Hydrangea can be used.

Hint 2
Roses can be added in different colors. Light pink and peach will make a blush effect.

Hint 3
If transporting the arrangement, use chicken wire over Oasis.

Materials

Mechanics
9" Clear Plastic Lomey Dish
½" Green Waterproof Florist Tape
1 Grande Oasis
½ Brick Oasis

Greenery
1 Bunch Green Pittosporum

Flowers
25 Stems White Hydrangea
12-24 Stems Roses
  ("Vendela and White Mondial")
12-24 White Carnations

Weddings — Small Design Concepts

Elizabeth and Scott Wedding
This bride wanted to use her church's classic urns which are quite small but needed to make a presence in a large space. A memorial candle for the Groom's mother was made to match.

Margaret and Thomas Wedding
Our bride and her mother wanted a garden look filled with southern Magnolia Ferns and blue and peach flowers to complement her red hair.
This design is created for a small altar.

Steps
See Basic Techniques: Classic Triangle

Materials

Greenery
½ Bunch Myrtle
1/3 Bunch Plumosa Ferns
6 Stems Magnolia
8 Stems Italian Ruscus

Flowers
Line: 10 Stems Blue Delphinium
16 Stems White Larkspur
10 Stems White Snapdragons

Focal: 12 Stems Rose "Tiffany"
6 Stems Rose "White O'Hara"

Supporting: 6 Stems White Lisianthus

Filler: 10 Stems Peach Spray Carnations
2 Bunches Orlaya

Steps
See Basic Techniques: Classic Triangle

Materials

Greenery
5 Stems Sasanqua
1/2 Bunch Pittosporum

Flowers
Line: 5 Stems White Larkspur

Focal: 3 Stems White Hydrangea
4 Stems Peach Spray Rose

Supporting: 2 Stems White Peonies

Filler: 2 Stems Mini Green Hydrangea
4 Stems Green Hypericum Berries

Weddings — Radial Designs

Materials

Mechanics
Ceramic boxes or green plastic dishes
Round dish in the middle (If a lot of material will be used in the middle)
Oasis to fit
Green tape

Greenery
1 Bunch Myrtle
1 Bunch Dark Green Pittosporum
1 Bunch Variegated Pittosporum
1 Bunch Salal

Flowers
Line: 10 Stems White Hybrid Delphinium
10 Stems Light Pink Snapdragons
10 Stems White Larkspur
10 Stems Pink Larkspur

Focal: 8 Stems "Pink Rose O'Hara" Garden Roses
15 Stems "Pink Mondial" Rose

Filler: 20 Stems White Hydrangea
14 Stems Cream "Vendela" Rose
10 Stems White Stock

Soft pink and white was the dream of this bride. She loved this fan shaped array of flowers. This radial design is one of our most popular designs for weddings. We have also included a few different color combinations for this design.

Steps

1. Set three to five boxes in a row.
   The middle container could be a round deeper dish.
2. Cover base with greenery.
3. Set line with Myrtle. Follow with Delphinium, Snapdragons, and Larkspur.
   Important to keep radial placement of all stems.
4. Add Hydrangea in lower half of arrangement in soft triangle shape.
5. Insert Roses starting with pink ones. Roses should have in and out movement in Hydrangea.
6. Use Stock to fill the gaps.

Blue Version

Materials Flowers
9 Stems Light Blue Hydrangea
9 Stems Mini Green Hydrangea
10 Stems Light Blue Delphinium
10 Stems White Snapdragons
10 Stems Bells of Ireland
1 Bunch White Lisianthus
15 Stems Rose "Super Green"
12 Stems Rose "Polo"
1 Pot Variegated Ivy

Deeper Pink Version

Materials Flowers
10 Stems Pink Snapdragons
9 Stems Pink Gladiolas
24 Stems Rose Pink Floyd
5 Stems Peony "Sarah Bernhardt"
5 Stems Peony "Pecher"
10 Stems Hydrangea "Antique Green"
20 Stems White Phlox
1 Bunch Variegated Pittosporum
1 Bunch Salal

Weddings

A Garden Altar

We love to create a natural garden look by grouping similar blooms. Flowers are placed in vertical groupings as if they are growing in nature. There is a slight radial nature within each grouping, but the overall design is not radial. Many special flowers are featured such as "café au lait", Dahlias, "Mother of Pearl", Roses and dutch Hydrangea. This design in soft blush is one of our favorites and can be done with a variety of color schemes. One of my favorites was a white one we did in January.

Steps

1. Put Oasis in boxes and tape down. Do not tape around the front of the box if possible. Soak.
2. Cover the base with Pittosporum.
3. Set the areas for taller elements of the design by grouping the Gladiolas, Snapdragons and Myrtle in taller areas. The center should have one substantial tall grouping. Be careful to balance the tall sections on each side. Place the flowers so that some are leaning out and tilting backwards.
4. Place the next largest and most important blooms, the café au lait Dahlias and dutch Hydrangea.
5. Insert the Roses using in and out placement of the stems.
6. Use the Salal and Leather Leaf at this point to accent the flowers in the tall area placing between the stems.
7. Insert Carnations to augment the Roses.
8. Use wheat celosia to support the tall areas and add softness.

Materials

Mechanics
Round Plastic Dish
4 Black Ceramic Boxes
1 Oasis Grande
6 Oasis Bricks
¼" Waterproof Tape

Greenery
Line: 1 Bunch Myrtle

Base: 2 Bunches Green Pittosporum
2 Bunches Variegated Pittosporum
1 Bunch Salal
1 Bunch Leather Leaf

Flowers
Line: 9 Stems Pink Gladiolas
9 Stems Pink Snapdragons
10 Stems Pink/Orange Snapdragons ("Talisman")
7 Stems Pussy Willow

Focal: 6 Stems Café Au Lait Dahlias
12 Stems "Mother of Pearl" Roses
5 Stems "Pink Cream" Dutch Hydrangea

Supporting: 4 Stems "Pink Mondial" Roses
7 Stems "Vendela" Roses

Filler: 8 Stems Peachy Beige Carnation
8 Stems "Lizzie" Carnations
1 Bunch Celosia Wheat Light Pink

Weddings — Iron Stands

This bride wanted a natural garden look to soften a very large space. She wanted to use sustainable materials as well. We used two iron stands each with 6 baskets. Half the baskets have potted Ivy. The others had plastic dishes with cut flowers. The Ivy can be reused for months. This design will become one of your favorites.

Steps

1. Put Oasis in liners. Oasis should be 3" over the rim. Tape around in cross pattern.
2. Green liners with basic greenery (save Seeded Eucalyptus until the end).
3. Place Ivy in alternating pots. Cover Ivy containers with Sheet Moss.
4. Put liners in baskets. If needed, use styrofoam to elevate. Cover baskets with Sheet Moss.
5. Place flowers starting with Hydrangea. Place loosely creating soft look.
6. Finish by adding Seeded Eucalyptus to flowers.

Materials

Mechanics
2 Garden stands: Free standing with baskets that can hold Ivy and flowers
Liners to fit baskets

Greenery
Pots of draping Ivy
Sheet Moss to cover Ivy base

Per liner:
- 1/3 Bunch Leather Leaf
- 1/3 Bunch Pittosporum
- 1/3 Bunch Salal
- 1/4 Bunch Variegated Pittosporum
- 1/4 Bunch Seeded Eucalyptus

Flowers
Per liner:
- 2 Stems White Hydrangea
- 3 Stems Peach "Lizzie" Carnations
- 5 Stems "Mother of Pearl" Rose
- 3 Stems "Vendela" Rose
- 1 Stem "White O'hara" Garden Rose
- 3 Stems Stock
- 1/3 Bunch White Statice

Weddings Sophie's Garden Wedding

Our bride wanted to have a garden themed wedding inspired by the fabric of her bridesmaids dresses. In this classic New England styled church, we created a garden setting by placing the flowers on a railing which was only 4" deep. This is a great way to use local blooming branches, Hydrangea and greenery. We paired matching wreaths on the entrance doors.

Steps

1. Measure the number of boxes required. We used white ceramic ones to match railing.
2. Insert pots of draping Ivy between the sections.
3. Follow the instructions for the Wedding: A Garden Altar Tall elements first – then focal – use others to support.

Materials

Mechanics
Ceramic Boxes or green plastic dishes
Oasis to fit

Greenery
1 Bunch Gardenia Greens
2 Bunches Leather Leaf
2 Bunches Dark Green Pittosporum
2 Bunches Myrtle
4 Pots of Ivy
Mood Moss to cover gaps

Flowers

Line: 10 Stems Apple Blossom Snapdragons
10 Stems Green Gladiolas
10 Stems Pink Snapdragons

Focal: 5 Stems Sarah Bernhardt Peony
5 Stems Coral Charm Peony
8 Stems Oakleaf Hydrangea
6 Stems "Sophie" Rose
4 Stems "Pink Floyd" Rose

Supporting Blooms: 6 Stems "Geraldine" Rose
8 Stems "Super Green" Rose

Filler: 8 Stems White Hydrangea
8 Stems Mini Green Hydrangea
8 Stems Light Pink Spray Carnations

Weddings — A Spring Fresh Wedding

This wedding happened late in April when flowers are in full bloom. The bride chose a color palette of white with pops of spring green, bright pink and peach. The family wanted to incorporate fresh garden greenery including their favorites of Ivy and Fern.
This wedding shows how all the pieces of ceremony flowers come together. Starting with the wreaths on the outside doors

Materials

Flowers
White Hydrangea
White Hybrid Delphinium
White Snapdragons
White Larkspur
White Freesia
White Lisianthus
White Carnations
Rose "White O'Hara"
Rose "Pink Mondial"
Rose "Pink O'Hara"
Rose "Sophie"
Rose "Vendela"
Rose "Mother of Pearl"
Mini Green Hydrangea
Peach Spray Carnation
Rose "Tiffany"

Weddings   Wedding Wreaths

The circle form of a wreath symbolizes the never-ending promise of love. They create a beautiful entrance to a wedding. Wreaths are a great way to say there is a wedding here and to welcome guests.

You will need one or two Oasis wreath forms (Note: 15" to 22" is usully appropriate for a door). When measuring, remember to add two inches to each side to account for the flowers and greenery that will be placed on the wreath.

For Instructions: See Basic Techniques: Wreath

Weddings   Pew Sprays

1/ Peach Version

Materials

Flowers

- 3 stems   White Larkspur
- 3 Stems   Rose "Vendela"
- 4 Stems   Spray Rose Porcelina
- 5 Stems   Queen Anne's Lace
- 5 Stems   White Freesia
- 3 Stems   Delphium "Sky Waltz"
- 2 Stems   Dusty Miller
- 2 Stems   Green Mum "Athos"
- Plumosa

Flowers cascading down pews finish the look of a beautiful wedding. When you open the door to a church, they say "Wedding". Added to glowing aisle candles, they take your breath away. "Wow! Beautiful!" is what we often hear guests say when they enter a church lined with floral sprays.

The pew sprays do not need to be placed on every pew. We like to place them on the front and rear pews and a few in between, budget permitting. They can also be used to mark the rows where the family is sitting. The sprays can be repurposed at the reception or a brunch. They make ideal table runners, mantel flowers, door sprays or mail box décor.

Here are some samples of pew sprays.
All follow the Basic Technique: Floral Sprays.

1/

2/ Classic white says wedding

Materials Flowers
- 1 Stem Italian Ruscus
- 1/3 Bunch Variegated Boxwood
- 1/2 Bunch Pittosporum
- 1/3 Bunch Leather Leaf
- 2 Stems White Hydrangea
- 3 Stems White Lisianthus
- 5 Stems Rose "White Mondial"
- 2 Stems White Larkspur

3/ Hot Pink and Soft Green

Materials Flowers
- 1 Stem Hydrangea "Antique Green"
- 5 Stems Snapdragons "Appleblossom"
- 3 Stems Rose "Pink Floyd"
- 2 Stems Spray Rose "Pink Majolica"
- 3 Stems Rose "Sweet Unique"
- 1/2 Bunch Leather Leaf
- 1/2 Bunch Pittosporum
- 1 Stem Italian Ruscus
- 5 Stems White Phlox

Hint 1
Greenery should radiate from the center of the cage.

Hint 2
For cascading look, use draping materials such as Ruscus and Ivy.

A shoot shall come out from the stock of Jesse,
and a branch shall grow out of his roots.
The spirit of the Lord shall rest on him,
the spirit of wisdom and understanding,
the spirit of counsel and might,
the spirit of knowledge and the fear of the Lord.
His delight shall be in the fear of the Lord.

Isaiah 11:1-3 (NRSV)

Christmas and Advent Introduction

Christmas is the celebration of the birth of Christ. Advent is a time of preparation and prayer for the coming of Christ. It is celebrated beginning four Sundays before Christmas. Evergreens such as Holly, Ivy and firs are common decorations used during the Advent and Christmas seasons.

From ancient times, evergreens have been used as winter decorations. Because they were the only plant material available, they were brought inside as decorations and a sign of spring in the midst of winter darkness.
Evergreens are also said to be symbolic of the promise of eternity that Christ brings.

During Advent, many churches decorate solely with greenery, adding berries as Christmas gets closer. Other churches will begin their Christmas decorations starting with the first Sunday in Advent.

Advent is a great time to experiment with using greenery only. Not only is greenery budget friendly, but it can also be fun to see what guild members may have in their gardens. We typically start Advent with local greenery from the church grounds and guild members homes. As Christmas nears we add more signs of the coming of Christmas such as Holly, Fir and Berries.

A Plan for Advent Greenery:

First Week of Advent
Local garden greenery

Second Week of Advent
Add Holly and Cedar

Third Week
Add Firs

Fourth Week
Add berries galore

Christmas and Advent Greenery

When to order

Wholesalers offer discounts for early orders of Christmas greenery. Usually the orders are due in October. Churches decorate beginning with the first Sunday in Advent so delivery should be around Thanksgiving. The Episcopal and Catholic churches decorate after the fourth Sunday in Advent. Most greenery is shipped in mid-November so it is quite old by Christmas. Work with your wholesaler to get a fresh shipment of greenery and wreaths towards the end of December.

How to Condition

Cut and place in water when possible. Christmas Fir likes cooler temperatures. Keep it in a cool dark place. If possible store in water in a cooler. The waxed box it is received in or large plastic bags make ideal storage containers. Mist with water every couple of days. We soak our Fir and wreaths over night when possible, which rejuvenates the Fir and extends its life. Large plastic tubs help with this process.

Guide to Christmas Greenery

Here are some options for greenery that are available in the Advent and Christmas seasons.

Yellows:
Aucuba, Variegated Boxwood, Bright Green Leaves, Golden/Yellow Deodor Cedar, Port Orford Cedar, Incense Cedar with yellow tips

Blue Grey:
Blue Atlas Cedar, Dusty Miller, Noble Fir, Bay Leaves, Eastern Red Cedar with Blue Berries (Berried Juniper), Carolina Sapphire Cypress, Eucalyptus

White Variegated:
Variegated Holly, Variegated Pittosporum

Bright Green:
Incense Cedar, Southern Long Leaf Pine, Leland Cypress, Cryptomeria japonica, Monterey Cypress (Tall + round cones)

Dark Greens:
Holly, English Boxwood, Camellia, Frasier Fir, Douglas Fir, Ivy

Berries:
Ilex verticillata, Holly Berries, Nandina Berries, Red Hypericum Berries

Hint
The part of the stem of fir that will go in Oasis should be stripped. Keeps Oasis from ripping up and hole from getting too big.

Incense Cedar | Frasier Fir | Noble Fir | Cypress

Carolina Sapphire | Juniper | Douglas Fir | Princess Pine | Blue Atlas Cedar

Christmas Special Flowers

Red is the color used most often in Christmas designs. Beautiful red berries are at their peak during Christmas. Red flowers are grown for the holiday. Red Charm Peonies, Red Lion Amaryllis and the full Corazon Roses are some of my favorites. Red Carnations and Spray Carnations add a frilly texture.

Consider these possible color combinations
- All red varying in texture
- Red and white
- Red and white with pops of a bright lime green
- Red, burgundy and peach
- All white and green

Here are some special flowers and berries that are available in the Christmas season

Amaryllis

Amaryllis, which is in season in the winter, is a beautiful flower to use for Christmas. Potted Amaryllis are lovely to mix with Poinsettias. People tend to shy away from using Amaryllis in designs because of its large stems that tend to split. Look at the instructions for using Amaryllis in Basic Techniques: Wiring and More. Using this technique you can use Amaryllis in a many of designs.

Holly

Traditionally Holly has been considered a symbol of Christ with its pointed ends representing the crown of thorns and the red berries representing drops of blood. In its full glory in December, Holly is commonly used in Christmas decorations. There are over 400 varieties of Holly.

Narcissus Paperwhites

Narcissus Paperwhites are fragrant plants forced to bloom for the Christmas season. They are a nice option if you are considering a touch of white in your designs. They typically are timed to bloom early in December so work with your wholesaler to get some later blooming ones for Christmas decorations.

Poinsettias

Poinsettias are the quintessential Christmas Flower. While red Poinsettias are the classic color for Christmas, there are over 100 varieties including pink, marbled, white, and salmon. Poinsettias grow in the wild from Mexico to Guatemala often reaching 10 to 15 feet in height. Tradition holds that Franciscan monks used Poinsettias as Christmas decorations in the 17th century.

They were introduced to the United States in 1832 by Joel Roberts Poinsett, the first United States Minister to Mexico and a botanist.

Buying Poinsettias:
Poinsettias are sold in many locations. We find it best to pre-order them from wholesalers or growers. The quality is better with fuller stems and more blooms. Work with your whole saler to get Poinsettias grown to your decorating time. Usually a better price can be obtained by ordering them in advance.

Using Poinsettias:
Poinsettias are best used in their planted form.
Buy baskets and ceramic pots that fit the typical 6" diameter of a poinsettia so they can be used without having to transfer and plant them.

To use Poinsettias in floral designs, we find that the following technique works well to insert them into arrangements and to keep them moist.

Steps

1. Make sure Poinsettias are moist or water the night before using.
2. Remove their pots and place the entire plant in a small plastic bag. (Put the plant, dirt, and roots in the bag).
3. Seal the bag with a rubber band.
4. In this form, Poinsettias can be tucked into designs.
5. To insert in an arrangement: put one garden stake on each side of the bag. Wrap with waterproof tape. Insert the stakes into the Oasis.
6. Poinsettias do not need much watering at this point, but check them. To water, pull back rubber band and use a narrow necked watering can. Careful not to over water!

Hint
Be sure to order some 4" pots of Poinsettias. Great to tuck into designs, but are hard to find if you do not pre-order them.

Christmas Advent Wreath

Flower Fact

Johann Hinrich Wichern, a German protestant pastor created the first Advent wreath in 1839. He built a large wooden wreath with four candles as a way to answer the perennial question from students in his mission school of how much longer to Christmas. Each week a new candle was lit to show how close it was to Christmas.

Materials

Mechanics
See Basic Techniques: Wreaths
¼" Waterproof Tape
Plastic Candle Holders
4 Advent Candles
1 Christmas Candle for center (optional)
15" Wreath Form

Greenery
Week 1: "From the Garden"
½ Bunch Green Pittosporum
½ Bunch Variegated Pittosporum
5 Stems Dwarf Yedda Hawthorne
5 Stems Nandina Leaves
3 Stems Camellia Leaves

Week 2: "Hints of Christmas"
6 Pieces Cypress
6 Pieces Crypotomeria

Week 3: "More Signs of Christmas"
6 Stems Dwarf Burford Holly
10 Stems Noble Fir Tips

Week 4: "Berries Galore"
10 Stems Red Hypericum Berries
5 Stems Nandina Berries

The Advent Wreath is used to mark the time before Christmas. The circular wreath form symbolizes eternal life and God's unending love for us. The candles symbolize the light of Christ coming into the world. The wreaths are used in churches and in homes throughout the season of Advent. Each week another candle is lit to symbolize the week of Advent. As Christmas gets closer and the light of Christ is nearer, more light shines as more candles are lit. The lighting of the wreath can be part of daily prayer in preparation for Christmas.

The candles on the wreath are lit in progression symbolizing hope, peace, joy and love. The candles can be purple or blue depending upon church tradition. Some churches use a rose candle on third week, the color of joy. A fifth candle, the Christ candle, can also be lit in the center.

We typically start decorating our Advent wreath the first week with basic garden greenery and add touches of Christmas as the weeks progress. The second week we add Holly and Cypress. The third week we add Christmas Fir. And finally on the fourth week we add loads of berries.

An Oasis ring is the best way to keep Advent greenery alive for the season. We use 15" and 21" forms at church. All the plant materials can be found in the garden. Look in Christmas tree lots where they are happy to give away bits and pieces of leftover branches. This technique works well for home Advent wreaths using a smaller 12" wreath form. The wreath forms with a full plastic bottom are nice as they will hold water to keep the Oasis moist. If the wreath is kept watered, it can last the entire Advent season. Be sure to spray heavily with water as the greenery will drink water through its leaves.

Steps

Week One:
1. Follow Basic Techniques for wreaths.
2. Wrap with thin waterproof tape leaving 3" gap between.
3. Insert candle holders in four spots evenly placed. Place center candle in middle if using.
4. Cover base with Pittosporum and Hawthorne so that all Oasis is covered.
5. Add Nandina and Camellia.

Week Two:
Add Crypotomeria and Cypress.
Week Three:
Add more Christmas like materials such as Noble Fir and Holly.
Week Four:
Add red berries galore!

Hint 1
Soak Fir for a few hours or overnight before using.

Hint 2
Water! Water!! Water!
The greenery must be watered to keep the Oasis moist.

Christmas Advent Altar

Altars for Advent use a variety of greenery most of which can be found in gardens. You can supplement with special Fir as the season of Advent progresses. We usually use local garden greenery for the first week adding Fir and Berries later.

This design would be for a third week of Advent altar using Christmas Fir. The color palette of a wintery blue and grey greenery was inspired by the lovely Cedar with Blue Berries. Dusty Miller was added to further emphasize the color scheme. The graceful curves of the Cedar set the shape which gently surrounds the cross. The photos on this page present a more traditional Christmas color palette.

Steps

1. Set the Oasis in the box. Chamfer the front edge.
2. Set the line with the tall pieces of Cedar. Insert outer edge pieces first. Add two pieces in the middle.
3. Cover the base with Pittosporum.
4. Add Cypress for texture contrast.
5. Add more greenery (Fir and Holly) to continue the line descending towards the cross.
6. Insert Dusty Miller in focal areas.
7. Add light touches of the Blue Atlas Cedar.

3rd week Advent
Materials
Mechanics
- 2 Black Ceramic Boxes
- ¼" Waterproof Tape
- 3 Blocks of Oasis

Greenery
- 6 Stems Noble Fir
- 6 Stems Blue Atlas Cedar
- 6 Stems Incense Cedar
- 5 Stems Red Cedar with blue berries
- 6 Stems Green Cypress
- 1 Bunch Green Pittosporum
- 6 Stems Dusty Miller
- 10 Stems Dwarf Burford Holly

Hint
Keep this altar watered and it can be used for the base of an arrangement for Christmas Eve. Add red flowers and voila you are done!

Christmas — Main Altar

Materials

Mechanics
See BasicTechniques: Classic Urn
Low Compote Style Container
2 Box Shaped Containers
2 Planters for Topiaries
½" Waterproof Tape
Chicken Wire

Floral Sprays:
See Christmas: Sprays Two Ways

Central Arrangement

Greenery
50' Mixed Fir and Cypress Roping
1 Bunch Green Pittosporum
5 Branches Magnolia
5 Branches Sasanqua
5 Branches Douglas Fir
4 Branches Blue Atlas Fir
Smilax

Flowers
8 Stems Peony "Henri Boxstoce"
12 Stems "Corazon" Red Rose
10 Stems "Freedom" Rose
10 Stems Red Carnations
7 Stems Red Leafless Ilex Berries
10 Stems Red Anthurium
5 Stems Red Spray Carnatiosn

Asymmetrical Arrangements

(Recipe for one side)
Greenery
1 Bunch Pittosporum
½ Bunch Boxwood
6 Stems Cypress
4 Branches Douglas Fir
1 Branch Altas Fir

Flowers
5 Stems Red Gerbers
8 Stems Red Spray Carnations
12 Stems Freedom Roses
6 Stems Red Carnations

Topiaries

See Basic Designs Topiaries
Greenery
1 Bunch Pittosporum
½ Bunch Boxwood
Mood Moss
Smilax

Flowers
24 Stems Red Rose Corazon
24 Stems Red Carnations
15 Stems Red Hypericum Berries

Brilliant monochromatic red makes a dramatic impact at Christmas. This Christmas design is a composition of different designs united by the color red. Flowers were grouped for a strong visual impact.
The first step was to drape the altar with a garland of Christmas greenery which framed the design.
The center arrangement used a Christmas tree inspired shape of all red blooms including winter blooming Peonies and deep red Corazon Roses. The central arrangement was flanked by two sets of topiaries and asymmetrical designs. Grey ceramic garden style containers were used to unite the look. Poinsettias in mossed pots and window boxes tied the reds together and extended the impact of red.
The look was replicated on the front chancel rail with swagged greenery roping and floral sprays.

Central Arrangement
Steps

1. Set Oasis in center urn. Cover with chicken wire.
2. Cover base of urn with Pittosporum.
3. Create a triangle shape with the Douglas Fir.
4. Place Magnolia in central area.
5. Set the line by grouping freedom Roses at top in triangular shape.
6. Reinforce the top section with Ilex.
7. Group Antherium on sides to create the lower portion of the triangle. Place at angle to cascade downward.
8. Place Peonies in center spacing to create a triangle.
9. Fill the gaps with the red Corazon Roses.
10. Sprinkle red Spray Carnations throughout.
11. Drape Smilax around base.
12. Add red Tulips and Atlas Blue cascading to each side to continue drape.

Asymmetrical Arrangements
Steps

These designs are asymmetrical to frame the center design
1. Green the base of arrangement.
2. Set the height with the Roses grouping in a triangular shape.
3. Place the Gerbers in a cascading pattern as the inside.
4. Use the Spray Carnations to create the shorter outer edge.
5. Fill the center section with Roses.
6. Intersperse Carnations and Boxwood.

Christmas

Classic Christmas Altar

Materials

Mechanics
5 Black Ceramic Boxes
¼" Waterproof tape

Greenery
Noble Fir Boughs and Tips
Scotch Pine
Nandina Branches and Clusters
1 Bunch Pittosporum

Flowers
11 Stems Red Leafless Ilex Berries
14 Stems "Freedom" Rose
14 Stems "Corazon" Rose
14 Stems Red Spray Carnations

This classic Christmas look was created in a series of boxes with Noble Fir. The design was used on the altar for Advent with simply greenery and berries. Red flowers were popped in the design on Christmas Eve.

Steps

1. Cover the base with Pittosporum.
2. Set the shape with the Noble Fir.
3. Fill with Cypress and Nandina.
4. Follow and accent the line with Ilex and Nandina Berries.
5. Insert Roses following shape of design.
6. Fill with Spray Carnations.

Christmas Window Box

Flickering candles in windows on Christmas Eve help to create the excitement of the coming of Christmas and the light of Christ. Many churches have nice window sills on which to place these arrangements. They do not take a lot of material and can be done ahead.

Steps

1. Soak Oasis and place in box. Tape if necessary but not across area where candle will be placed.
2. Place hurricane globe in center of Oasis in box. Push globe into Oasis. Use wooden picks around edges to hold globe in place.
3. Cover base with Pittosporum.
4. Insert greenery in radial pattern starting with Fir and Camellia.
5. Place Spray Carnations and Berries.
6. Insert pillar candle and light when ready.

Materials

Mechanics
One box to fit the window
Hurricane Globe
Pillar Candle (or wax battery powered candle)
4" wooden picks
Oasis to fit box

Greenery
8 Stems Red Hypericum Berries (could substitute Holly and Nandina Berries)
5 Stems Red Spray Carnations

From the Garden
1/3 Bunch Green Pittosporum
1/3 Bunch Variegated Pittosporum
6 Pieces Dwarf Burford Holly
1 Branch Camellia
2 Branches Cedar
2 Branches Elaeagnus

Christmas Floral Sprays

Two different red options for pew sprays. One draping design looks beautiful on a tall aisle candle. The other one is appropriate for attaching directly to pews. Lots of this material can be found in gardens to keep the cost down. The variety of Christmas greenery including Fir, Cypress and Holly that make this design sing Christmas carols as parishioners enter the church.

Version 1: Recipe for a Smaller Design

Version 2: Draping Red Spray with a Southern Twist

Steps

1. Follow Basic Techniques for pew sprays.
2. Cover base with Pittosporum, Boxwood and Cypress.
3. Create teardrop shape with Noble Fir tips inserting one longer. Let the long greenery set the drape of the spray.
4. Insert Southern Smilax draping and winding it around the spray.
5. Place Corazon Roses in triangle pattern.
6. Place the Nandina Berries draping at the bottom.
7. Insert red standard and spray Carnations in between and with one descending downward.
8. Insert Hypericum Berries and incense Cedar as filler.

Materials

Mechanics
One small cage

Greenery
½ Bunch Leather Leaf
½ Bunch Green Pittosporum
¼ Bunch Seeded Eucalyptus

From the Garden
4 Stems Nandina Leaves and Berries
4 Stems Holly
2 Stems Camellia

Flowers
5 Stems "Corazon" Red Rose
4 Stems Red Spray Carnations
3 Stems Pussy Willow

Materials

Mechanics
See Basic Techniques: Pew Sprays
One large cage
Bindwire
Waterproof Tape

Greenery
½ Bunch Green Pittosporum
4 Stems Noble Fir Tips
1 Stem Red Cedar (with Blue Berries)
1 Stem Carolina Sapphire Cedar
6 Pieces Dwarf Burford Holly
2 pieces Smilax

Flowers
3 Stems "Corazon" Red Rose
3 Stems "Freedom" Rose
2 Stems Red Spray Rose
3 Stems Red Spray Carnations
3 Stems Red Carnations
3 Stems Red Hypericum Berries.

Hint
Cut large woody stems in a point for a better hold.

Christmas Wreaths

Christmas wreaths are a must for the entrance to any church at Christmas. The evergreens and shapes are a sign of the eternal life that is promised through the birth of Christ. We have 9' and 6' lighted wreaths on the outside of our buildings. Shining down Peachtree street, our major thoroughfare, they are a welcoming beacon. We usually order dozens of additional wreaths to use throughout the church.

Wreaths can be used in their plain evergreen form with a bright red bow or with additional decorations. Order premade wreaths in October when Christmas Greens are discounted. Plain Noble Fir wreaths are a good starting point for wreaths that will be decorated. Different kinds of evergreen can be added to give depth and contrast such as Berried Cedar or Blue Cypress. The décor could be fruit, Pine Cones, dried Hydrangea, dried fall materials, nuts, berries, Christmas ornaments, faux birds and more. All kinds of ribbon can be used to coordinate with the look and colors of your Christmas plan. Start with a plain wreath and let your imagination go.

Wreaths can also be made in Christmas colors out of greenery and flowers. Follow the wreath instructions in Basic Techniques: Floral Wreaths. Roses, Carnations Spray Carnations, Spray Roses, Berries and all sorts of Christmas greenery make a beautiful wreath.

A word on faux wreaths. We try to avoid using faux material but Christmas wreaths are one exception. Purchasing some faux wreaths is a good cost saving measure because they can be used year-after-year. Faux pre-lit wreaths work nicely in outdoors locations. They are also good in locations where wreaths will need to stay for multiple weeks. The materials used to make these wreaths are improving and are fairly realistic. They do require fluffing each year so they do not look like they just came out of a box.

Follow this recipe for a Red Christmas Floral Wreath:

Materials

Mechanics
18" Diameter Wreath

Greenery
½ Bunch Green Boxwood
1 Bunch Pittosporum
5 Branches Holly with berries
8 Stems Christmas Fir

Flowers
15 Stems Red Carnations
10 Stems Red Spray Carnations
12 Stems Red Corazon Roses
10 Stems Red Spray Carnations
10 Stems Red Hypericum Berries

Christmas Draping Ivy Wall

Gudrun Cottenier, author and floral instructor taught us this technique on one of our European tours. She led us in a workshop decorating her 18th century church in her town of Mater, Belgium. We used Ivy in all kinds of ways as a cost-effective means of decorating. This technique uses common Ivy to create a dramatic effect in a large space for very little cost. This technique could be used for Easter or Christmas. The draping Ivy could be used anywhere where there is room to drape such as a pulpit, choir stalls, balcony, or chancel rail. We have modified the concept using Elaeagnus, which grows abundantly in our region, to create a base for the Ivy and a silvery undertone.

Steps

Steps 1 through 4 can be done before arranging day

1. Attach eye hooks on back of area where cages will be attached.
2. Soak Oasis and place in cages. Tape around cage placing on top of plastic bars.
3. Double bind wire and place on each end. Be sure to go through cage and holes. (See Basics: Cages)
4. Insert Pittosporum to cover cage. Make sure to cover edges, better to cover with greenery on a flat surface rather than standing on a ladder. Keep moist if doing ahead.
5. Hang cages wrapping multiple times around eye hooks.
6. Insert Elaeagnus creating the base of the drape. Vary the lengths. Take shorter pieces and layer on the top to create a fullness on top.
7. Layer Ivy over and in between Elaeagnus. To make it easier to insert, cut the ends of the Ivy in diagonal points.
8. Insert Carnations, Spray Carnations and Berries in an up and down pattern keeping most flowers in band area of cage. Let a few Spray Carnations drape downward.
9. Insert Lilies in key focal points at the end so as to not break petals off the blooms.

Materials

Mechanics
8 Large Cages
½" Waterproof Tape
Bind wire
Eye Hooks
Ladders
Tub for Ivy

Greenery from the Garden:
This is approximate as the size of the stems will vary
4 Bunches Green Pittosporum
48 Stems Long draping Ivy
 (Look for full leaves and nice tips)
24 Stems Long Elaeagnus
 (Look for nice tips)

Flowers
25 Stems Red Hypericum Berries
 (could substitute Holly and Nandina Berries)
20 Stems Red Spray Carnations
50 Stems Red Carnations
10 Stems Red Asiatic Lilies

Hint 1
This design can be done with only Ivy.

Hint 2
In December, Ivy is a nice green and firm. Cut it the day before using and spritz with water leaving it in a tub overnight outdoors (if it is not freezing).

Shout with joy to the Lord,
all you lands,
lift up your voice,
rejoice and sing

Psalm 98

Easter Introduction

Alleluia! Easter is a time of a joyful celebration of new life. The worship experience is enhanced by glorious flowers and music. The Easter Festival focuses on the joy and promise of the resurrection and a new life. Easter flowers should be magnificent and abundant. Set in the spring time, Easter is surrounded by all the elements of new life emerging. A time to celebrate the resurrection of life. Spring flowers are the central feature of the Easter floral design.

My favorite part of Easter is the sunrise service, the Great Vigil. The Great Vigil of Easter marks the passage from Lent to Easter and Christ's Passover from death to life. At our Cathedral we have a huge bonfire outside. We then enter the church in the dark. The smell of Lilies and fresh flowers permeates the darkness. Flickers of white from the Lilies give hints of what is to come. As the sun slowly rises, the full glory of the colors and flowers of Easter emerges.

Easter is celebrated with a glorious array of flowers. Flowers adorn the altar areas, doorways, columns, street signs and the entrances to churches. Easter is a time to pull out all the stops. Place baskets of Lilies on entrance tables in all hallways, adorn the area around the cross, pews and columns. Many churches also have a tradition of flowering a cross. Parishioners are invited to place flowers on a cross.

Bright and vibrant palettes express the joy of Easter. There are a number of color options. As a festival, the traditional color is white. Adding a touch of yellow to the white flowers can make a beautiful design celebrating a new beginning and the regal glory of Christ. A palette of pastels reflects the softness of new life. Many churches are faced with bright red or blue carpets. Incorporate touches of red Tulips or Blue Hydrangea to subtly tie in those colors.

Color Options:
All White
White and Yellow
Bright:
Yellow, Hot Pink, Orange, Purple, Blues, and Bright Green
Pastel:
Soft pink and blue, peach, lavender, and white

The date of Easter rotates each year. We always start by finding out what will be blooming locally at that time. Spring blooming bulbs and branches are all possibilities. When it is March, the Daffodils are popping up in our area. In early April we have the Dogwood in bloom. As a symbol of new life, Dogwood is especially appropriate to use during Easter. Bulbs can include Daffodils, Narcissus, Tulips and Hyacinth. Tulips remind me of Easter. We are almost certain to include them. Branches depend on the timing of Easter. In its early dates, blooming cherry abounds followed by pear and double blooming cherry. Later in the season Dogwood branches can be used.

Gardens seem an especially appropriate theme for Easter. Christ met the disciples in the Garden of Gesthame. Try creating a garden for Easter. Cut flowers can be used to create a garden in front of an altar, as a back drop or in an entranceway. A garden can be created with trees and shrubs which will eventually be planted in the church grounds. Tuck potted Easter Lilies into both designs. Use plenty of Moss. Find one huge rock to symbolize the stone in front of the tomb.

The Lily is traditionally used as a flower for Easter. The slender, trumpet shaped Longiflorum Lily is the quintessential Lily used. Throughout history, graceful and snow white Lilies have been used as a symbol of purity, innocence and fertility, Early paintings show the Angel Gabriel giving an Easter Lily to Mary. Mary found Lilies when she went to Jesus's tomb. Cut liies can be used in arrangements. Potted Lilies are nice to tuck into designs, put in baskets, or plant outside in pots.

Why does the date of Easter Change?
The death of Christ occurred around Passover. Passover is set according to the date of the spring equinox. The date of Easter is traditionally set on the Sunday following the first full moon of that equinox. It can fall anywhere between March 22nd and April 25th with the Gregorian Calendar

Easter Tips & Tricks

Blooming Branches:
To force blooming branches: Get them on Monday. Put in a sunny spot or room. Fresh cut with sharp ratchet clippers and put in deep water. Recut mid-week.

Daffodils:
Must be kept separate because they give off a gas that cause other flowers to wilt.
1. Put in a separate vase and tuck in the design.
2. Leave in bulb brushing off the dirt and tuck in the design.
3. Leave in pots or put in plastic bags.

Easter Lilies:
1. Get Easter Lilies early, probably Monday of Easter week.
2. Look for Lilies that have white in their buds. Green ones will take over a week to open.
3. Most cut Lilies are shipped tight in the bud. If they are very tight, fresh cut them and put them in warm water. Put them in a warm room or outside If the weather is warm. Fresh cut them every other day and put in more fresh warm water.
4. Order dark green wrappers for potted Lilies.
5. Buy containers that hold one potted Lily or multilples. They are an easy way to display Lilies and can be reused each year. Mix with Ferns and cover edges with Moss.

Tulips:
Grow 1" per day and turn towards the sun.
1. Should be kept in the cooler as long as possible.
2. Clean torn or decayed leaves off stems. Rewrap in plastic and store in refrigerator.
3. No Refrigerator? Store in cool place or ask your wholesaler to keep them for you until Friday.
4. Some say putting a wire in the stem just below the head keeps the Tulips from turning.
5. Best: Place Tulips where you do not mind them turning towards the light.

Flower Facts

Longiflorum Lily: Imagine the challenge growers face timing Lilies to all bloom perfectly for one specific day which rotates every year!

Symbolism of the Dogwood: The shape of the Dogwood is similar to a cross. Look closely at the little rust colored marks on the edges of the petals. Could they be symbolic of the blood of Christ?

Easter Main Altar

For Easter and other festivals we create an expansive altar arrangement. For this Easter we placed a low design below the cross and two classic arrangements on each side. We put the more intense colors and special flower concentrated in the center urn. The side urns are accent pieces repeating the color scheme and flowers.

Steps See Classic Urn Design instructions

Materials

Mechanics
1 Low Urn
2 Taller Urns
2 Grande Oasis
1 Designer Oasis
Plastic Liners to fit containers

Center Arrangement
Greenery
1 Bunch Leather Leaf
1 Bunch Green Pittosporum
10 Stems Sword Fern

Flowers
Line: 7 Stems Blue Delphinium Hybrid
7 Stems Pink Snapdragons
6 Stems White Larkspur
Focal: 5 Stems "Coral Charm" Peonies
5 Stems "Amsterdam" Roses
3 Stems Lily Longiflorum
Filler: 7 Stems "Lizzie" Carnations
10 Stems "Sky Waltz" Delphinium
8 Stems Hot Pink Stock

Side Urns Recipe for one urn
Greenery
1 Bunch Leather Leaf
1 Bunch Green Pittosporum
10 Stems Sword Fern
1 Bunch Deflexus

Flowers
Line: 5 Stems Peach Gladiolas
7 Stems Blue Delphinium Hybrid
5 Stems Pink Snapdragons
6 Stems White Larkspur
6 Stems Bells of Ireland
Focal: 6 Stems "Tiffany Rose"
3 Stems "Amsterdam" Roses
3 Stems Lily Longiflorum
Filler: 7 Stems "Lizzie" Carnations
5 Stems White Stock
4 Stems Hot Pink Stock
5 Stems Mini Green Hydrangea

Easter — Garden Altar Base

The goal of this design is to create the look of a miniature garden with materials growing in natural groupings. Greenery is used to unite the pieces.

Steps

1. Insert Oasis into boxes. Tape across lengthwise.
2. Set up boxes with Oasis across base of altar. It is o.k. to leave gaps.
3. Place potted Lilies evenly spaced between boxes.
4. Green base with basic greenery to cover
5. Add elements of tall greenery grouping tall elements in three to five groups. Leave low sections in between.
6. Add Fern in natural growing placement to emphasize the taller elements. Allow some to drape along the lower edge.
7. Accent with greenery from the garden such as solomon's seal.
8. Insert line flowers in sections with tall greenery.
9. Place larger flowers in staggered heights .
10. Accent shape with Tulips.
11. Fill areas with Daisies, Stock and other flowers.
12. Sprinkle base with groupings of accent flowers. (Sweet William)

Materials

Mechanics
6 Rectangular ceramic boxes
9 Oasis bricks (1 ½ per box)
Waterproof Tape

Greenery
This is a great design to use bits and pieces from your garden
2 Bunches Pittosporum
2 Bunches Leather Leaf
10 Stems Holly Fern (From the garden)
2 Bunches Leather Leaf
1 Bunch Italian Variegated Pittosporum
8 Stems Solomon Seal
10 Stems Sword Fern

Flowers
3 Pots Longiflorum Lilies
10 Stems Pink Orange Snapdragons
7 Stems Blue Hybrid Delphinium
10 Stems Peach Gladiolas
10 Stems Bells of Ireland
10 Stems Sky Waltz Delphinium
10 Stems Lavender Stock
10 Stems Coral French Tulips
10 Stems Allium
7 Stems Peach Gerber Daisies
5 Stems Pink Hydrangea
5 Stems Blue Hydrangea
1 Bunch Lavender Daisies
1 Bunch Lavender Tulips
1 Bunch Hot Pink Sweet William
4 Stems Light Pink Spray Carnations

Hint 1
Leave open sections of negative space.

Hint 2
Have varying heights.

Hint 3
Group flowers by type.

Easter Door or Column Baskets

Steps

Mechanics

Can be done in advance

1. Find long basket, any shape will do. Attach picture frame gauge wire the length needed to hang.
2. Drill small holes in four corners of plastic dish.
3. Fold bind wire in half and Insert into holes.
4. Place brick or heavy object into bottom of basket.
5. Fill with lightweight packing material.
6. Fit dish on top of basket. Use dry Oasis or recycled styrofoam to fill gaps and make tight. Attach to sides of basket with bind wire.
7. Cut chicken wire to fit top of cage.
8. Secure with bind wire on one side.
9. Soak Oasis and put in dish.
10. Cover with chicken wire and attach with bind wire on opposite side.

Flowers

1. Cover Oasis with basic greenery such as Salal and Pittosporum.
2. Add draping and tall greenery such as Holly Fern, Sword Fern, and Variegated Lily Grass.
3. Insert line flowers into a fan shape staggering placement to create depth.
4. Place focal flowers such as Lilies and Roses.
5. Add filler such as Baby's Breath, Daisies, or Spray Carnations.
6. Hang and fill dish with water.

Materials

Mechanics
Long basket
Plastic Dish to fit top
Bind Wire
Foam peanuts
White Styrofoam packing material
Brick (or rock to fit bottom of basket)
Chicken Wire
Picture Frame Wire
One Brick of Oasis
Drill

Greenery

Draping: Holly Fern (from the garden)
Sword Fern
Variegated Lily Grass

Filler: Salal
Leather leaf
Florida Ruscus

Flowers

Line: Sky Waltz Delphinium
Sea Waltz Delphinium
Hot Pink Snapdragons

Focal: Longiflorum Lilies
Rose "Pink Floyd"

Filler: Lavender Daisies

Hint
Keep your eye out for nice vertically shaped baskets. Always buy in sets of even numbers. These are hard to find so start your search early!

Easter Pulpit

Easter and Christmas are two times during the year when we decorate the pulpit. The decorations can range from simple greenery to heavy flowers or a combination. The décor can be placed just around the top of the pulpit or draping down the sides.

Steps

1. Measure the length of pulpit and calculate how many cages you need.
2. Soak and put Oasis in cages.
3. Tape around each cage one time. Be sure to attach on top of plastic cage material.
4. Attach first cage to top of pulpit. Place an eyehook on the backside of the pulpit to thread the wire though.
5. Connect other cages with zip ties. Make one loop on one and connect it to the other cage with another loop.

Hint
These steps can be done well in advance. (Wait to soak the Oasis!)

Materials

Mechanics
4 Large Oasis Cages
2 Large Oasis cages
Oasis for cages
Waterproof tape
Zip ties
Bark Covered Wire

Greenery
6 Stems Italian Ruscus
1 Bunch Deflexus
10 Stems Swordfern
2 Bunches Leather Leaf
2 Bunches Variegated Pittosporum
1 Bunch Salal

Flowers
8 Stems "Free Spirit" Rose
8 Stems "Amsterdam" Rose
6 Stems "Pink Floyd" Rose
6 Stems Longiflorum Lilies
6 Stems White Larkspur
10 Stems "Lizzie" Carnations
10 Stems Light green Carnations
10 Stems White Spray Carnations
10 Stems Peach Hypericum Berries
4 Stems Light Pink Spray Carnations

6. Place line green on bottom to create a tapered end to the garland.
7. Green cages with Pittosporum and other greening material. Be sure to bridge gaps with greenery. Should be heavier towards cage tapering outward.
8. Add a fluffy greenery to soften the edges.
9. Place focal flowers (Easter Lilies) in strategic spots. Clustering at top is very effective.
10. Add next largest flowers spreading out evenly.
11. Add filler flowers and final touches of greenery like Sword Fern.

Alternatives
1. Use only cages on top of pulpit.
2. Stagger lengths of draping. Longer in front, longer in back or alternating.
3. Buy premade garland for top of rails to make it go quickly. Plumosa and Springereii Garland are an inexpensive combination. Tuck in flowers in tubes.

Easter Flowering Cross

Have a large wooden cross made to fit your space. The cross can be placed outside or in an entry way. Once you have the mechanics set up, you can use this form over and over again. We find it best to "Green the Cross" as a base for the flowers. This can be done days ahead. We provide basic flowers because Easter morning is busy enough. You can order as many flowers as your budget allows. Invite your parishioners to bring cuttings from their gardens too.

Steps

1. Find a carpenter to make a cross to fit your space.
2. Insert cross into christmas tree stand.
3. Attach backs of cages to cross with screws.
4. Insert soaked Oasis pieces. Put covers on cages. Secure with tape or zip ties.
5. Cover with greenery.
6. Place Lilies around bottom. Cover base with Moss.
7. Set up buckets with cut flowers near the cross.
8. Invite parishioners to place flowers on the cross as they enter or leave.

Materials

Mechanics
Large wooden cross
Cages to fit your cross.
  (We used 10 Large Cages, 12 small, and 4 square)
Christmas Tree Stand
Box to elevate (if needed)

Greenery
6 Bunches Pittosporum
3 Bunches Variegated Pittosporum
6 Bunches Leather Leaf
10 Stems Aspidistra
1 Box Mood Moss
1 Box Sheet Moss

Flowers
6 Pots Longiflorum Lilies
9 Stems Easter Lilies
16 Stems Mini Green Hydrangea
12 Stems "Free Spirit" Roses
24 Stems "Amsterdam" Roses
12 Stems "Tiffany" Roses
12 Stems White Daisies
12 Stems Lavender Daisies
20 Stems Purple Spider Mums
24 Stems Light Green Carnations
24 Stems Pink Carnations
24 Stems Peach Carnations

Hint

We find it best to set out baskets with flowers precut to the correct length to insert. It is a really fun job on Easter morning to greet everyone and help them decorate the cross.

Easter Kneeling Altar

Materials

Mechanics
2 White Ceramic Boxes
3 Oasis bricks
¼" Waterproof Tape

Greenery
6 Stems Holly Fern
½ Bunch Variegated Pittosporum
½ Bunch Leather Leaf

Flowers
5 Pots Easter Lilies
8 Stems Pink Snapdragons
12 Stems Blue Delphinium "Sea Waltz"
6 Stems Green Carnations
10 Stems Pink Tulips
10 Stems Peach Rose "Tiffany"

The act of kneeling in front of an altar was the inspiration for this design of an Easter altar. The Easter Lilies were placed to give the sense of the movement of kneeling.

The design was created with bits and pieces of leftover flowers from the other bunches of flowers ordered for Easter. Potted Lilies were cut and their angles and linear forms used to create the desired angles. The Blue Delphinium, pink Snapdragons and Holly Ferns were used to reinforce this line.

Steps

1. Set the Oasis in dishes. Tape down. Chamfer the front edge.
2. Cover Oasis with variegated Pittosporum and Leather Leaf.
3. Set the line with the Lilies.
4. Reinforce line with Holly Fern, Delphinium and Snapdragons.
5. Place Roses in central focal area.
6. Fill with Tulips and Carnations.

Easter Garland

Use this technique to create the effect of a garland without the expense and time. It takes very little mechanics. You use four Oasis cages to create a frame that looks like a garland. This design works best against a flat surface.

Use this technique to frame doors, windows, welcome signs, front railings and pulpits. Look around for places to frame.

The following recipe will complete one frame for one side of the chancel rail. You can use as many varieties as budget permits.

Steps

1. Put Oasis in cages. Soak.
2. Tape around cage one time. Be sure to attach tape on top of plastic lines on cages.
3. Attach to top and sides with either zip ties or heavy bark wire. Leave gap between which will be filled with greenery.
4. Use Italian Ruscus to set the line in "L" shape (or 90° angle) connecting in the middle.
5. Reinforce the Ruscus line with a second piece of Ruscus on each side.
6. Green cages with Pittosporum and other greening material. Be sure to bridge gaps with greenery. This should be heavier towards cage tapering outward.
7. Place focal flowers (Easter Lilies) in corners.
8. Reinforce the line with line flowers (Snaps, Larkspur) and Spray Carnations.
9. Drape Spray Carnations. Add next largest flowers. (Roses)
10. Fill with remaining flowers.
11. Add soft deflexus to soften greenery line.

Materials

Mechanics
2 Large Oasis Cages
2 Small Oasis cages
Oasis for cages
Waterproof tape
Zip ties
Bark Covered Wire

Greenery
8 Stems Italian Ruscus Long
2 Bunches Green Pittosporum
12 Stems Sword Ferns
1 Bunch Deflexus
½ Bunch Variegated Italian Ruscus
½ Bunch Variegated Boxwood
½ Bunch Salal

Flowers
8 Stems Easter Lilies (For corners)
6 Stems "Pink Floyd" Rose
5 Stems "Free Spirit" Rose
10 Stems Coral "Amsterdam" Rose
10 Stems Peach Hypericum Berries
5 Stems Peach "Tiffany" Rose
5 Stems Pale Green Carnations
5 Stems Mini Green Carnations
5 Stems Pale Pink Spray Carnations

Hint
You can add more cages to make a fuller look but it is amazing how full you can make this look with just four small cages.

Easter Processional Cross

Processional crosses are often decorated for Easter. Use bits and pieces of the flowers you are using elsewhere.

Steps

1. Slice top off of Iglu to make it less deep.
2. Wrap one time around with waterproof tape.
3. Tie bind wire through holes on each side.
4. Soak Oasis.
5. Use Pittosporum to cover Iglu paying attention to edges.
6. Insert Italian Ruscus and Orchids in a diagonal. (You may not need entire length)
7. Use Florida Ruscus to emphasize line and add dimension in the middle. (cut in pieces)
8. Insert Spray Roses.
9. Use limonium and statice to lightly fill gaps and to repeat diagonal line.

Hint 1
Be careful not to get too heavy with the flowers or it will overwhelm the cross.

Hint 2
Easter liies can be used for Easter morning.

Materials

Mechanics
Oasis Iglu Small
Bindwire
Processional Cross

Greenery
2 Italian Ruscus Tips
3 Florida Ruscus
Bits of Pittosporum

Flowers

Line: 2 Stems White Dendobrium Orchids

Focal: 1 Stem White Majolica Spray Rose
1 Stem White Vivianne Spray Rose

Filler: 2 Stems White Limonium
2 Stems White Statice

Easter Paschal Candle

A new Paschal candle is lit each year at Easter at the Easter Vigil service. The Paschal candle symbolizes the coming of Christ into the world. It remains in the sanctuary through the 50 days of Easter and is lit at baptisms and funerals throughout the year. Since it is a special part of the Easter service, it is often decorated for Easter. Smaller tighter blooms and greenery work best. We create our own wreath forms out of chicken wire as premade wreath forms are often not correctly sized for the candle.

Steps

1. Create a ring out of chicken wire to fit around the stand.
2. Insert small sections of Oasis foam. Insert Moss between pieces to make round shape.
3. Soak Oasis.
4. Cover base with dwarf yedda Hawthorne or small leaf greenery.
5. Add touches of Variegated Italian Pittosporum and Seeded Eucalyptus to lighten.
6. Insert Roses as focal elements.
7. Follow with white majolica Spray Roses and Scabiosa.
8. Fill with Hypericum Berries.
9. Add Scabiosa buds for looseness.

Materials

Mechanics
Small pieces of Oasis
Chicken Wire and Bindwire

Greenery
2 Stems Italian Variegated Pittosporum
Bits Seeded Eucalyptus
3 Stems Dwarf Yedda Hawthorne

Flowers
Focal: 6 Stems Peach Rose "Tiffany"
3 Stems White Majolica Spray Rose

Filler: 10 Stems Pink Scaboiosa with buds
5 Stems Pink Hypericum Berries

> When the day of Pentecost had come,
> they were all together in one place.
> And suddenly from heaven there came
> a sound like the rush of a violent wind,
> and it filled the entire house where
> they were sitting.
> Divided tongues, as of fire,
> appeared among them, and a tongue
> rested on each of them.
> All of them were filled with the Holy Spirit
> and began to speak in other languages,
> as the Spirit gave them ability.
>
> Acts 2:1-4 NRSV

Other festivals

Pentecost

Many other special days occur during the church year. A flower church flower calendar should be prepared at the beginning of each year so that you know the upcoming flower needs. The chart called Church Flower Colors by the Season will be helpful to begin the planning process. Special feast days such as Palm Sunday, Pentecost and Patron Saints Days have their own particular colors and plant materials.

Baptisms and funerals are considered Feast Days in many churches and have their own flower requirements. Individual churches will also have special events such as anniversaries. This chapter highlights some of the special days with some information and inspiration for floral designs.

Some call this day the beginning or birthday of the church. The apostles and others were gathered together when the Holy Spirit suddenly appeared as tongues of flame and descended upon some of those present as Jesus had promised. By speaking other languages, the disciples were symbolizing that the gospel was for the world to share.

The traditions celebrating Pentecost vary, but they typically involve the color of red and images of flames. We have provided two examples of flowers for Pentecost.

Pentecost — Altar of Flames

The goal of this design is to create a sense of flames. The look and color palette should be similar to a flame with yellow, orange and red. Touches of blue are added to reflect the center blue in a flame. Tropical flowers are perfect for this design. Birds of Paradise with their feather plumes and blue interiors look like flames. The yellow Spider Mums mimic sparks. Rose "High and Magic" with its red edges looks like it is burning around the edges.

Steps

1. Place dishes and Oasis to fit your space. We wedged a plastic dish behind the cross.
2. Place monster leaves in corners and center in a fan pattern
3. Cover with greenery to create a base shape. Group together the different types for maximum impact.
4. Place birds of paradise to create three areas of "flames" on the ends and in the middle.
5. Reinforce the flame with ginger and Gladiolas descending downward in height.
6. Create a center flame with red Antherium.
7. Fill low with intense yellow-orange Rose and pin cushion.
8. Add touches of yellow with Lilies and Spider Mums.
9. Insert Blue Delphinium towards the center of each grouping.

Materials

Mechanics
4 Black Ceramic Boxes
One plastic green dish
7 Regular Bricks Oasis
¼" Waterproof Tape

Greenery
1 Bunch Pittosporum
1 Bunch Variegated Pittosporum
6 Stems Acuba
1 Bunch Variegated Boxwood
1 Bunch Salal
7 Stems Medium Monstera Leaves

Flowers
10 Stems Yellow Gladiolas
11 Stems Birds of Paradise
6 Stems Red Ginger.
14 Stems Rose "High and Magic"
4 Stems Protea Pin Cushion Orange
4 Stems Yellow Spider Mums
3 Stems Yellow Lilies
5 Stems Red Antherium
15 Stems Sea Waltz Delphinium

Hint 1
Balance the more expensive tropical flowers with budget friendly flowers such as Spider Mums and Roses. Order tropical by the stem.

Hint 2
When ordering think of order by the number of groups of flames. For example, in this section there are three sets of flames.

Pentecost Single Design

Materials

Mechanics
1 White Ceramic Box
1 ½ Regular Bricks Oasis
¼" Waterproof Tape

Greenery
with a touch of yellow works well
1 Bunch Pittosporum
3 Stems Acuba
7 Stems Holly Fern

Flowers
7 Stems Birds of Paradise
5 Stems "High and Magic" Rose
3 Stems Yellow Spider Mums
3 Stems LA Hybrid Lily "Sunset"
3 Stems Red Antherium
10 Stems Red Carnations
5 Stems Sea Waltz Delphinium

This is another version of a flame design for an area needing a single arrangement. The powerful impact of the flame-like Birds of Paradise is shown here. Lily "Sunset" with its orange color and red tips is another Pentecost favorite.

Steps

1. Set Oasis in container and tape in place.
2. Cover base with Pittosporum and Aucuba.
3. Set Holly Fern in triangle pattern with three in the center and two draping on each side.
4. Place birds in flaming pattern.
5. Insert Lilies in center section.
6. Place red Antherium and Yellow Spider Mums in center for maximum impact.
7. Reinforce shape and color with high and magic Roses and red Carnations.

Funeral

On the Wings of Angels

Many Christians consider funerals and memorial services to be "Feast Days" because they are celebrations centered on the resurrection of Jesus. These services are characterized by "joy mixed with grief".

While we rejoice that one we loved has entered into the nearer presence of our Lord, we sorrow in sympathy with those who mourn.

BCP 507

This mixed sense of emotions is expressed in this prayer for the departed
All of us go down to the dust; yet even at the grave we make our song: Alleluia, alleluia, alleluia.

BCP

Beautiful flowers on the altar are part of the celebration as they would be at Easter. White flowers are often used, as white is typically the color of feast days. However brightly colored flowers or seasonal ones are also celebratory.

Many traditions have elaborate funerals and flowers. Flowers for funerals are often done by outside florists. Certainly, an array of flowers are delivered to the church in memory of the deceased from professional florists including baskets of potted plants, standing sprays, vase arrangements, and wreaths. Casket sprays are a tradition in some churches. These are typically done by professional florists as well.

Whether church flower guilds arrange the flowers on the altar for funerals and memorial services varies considerably from church to church. At our church we arrange all the altar flowers for funerals. I would commend others to consider offering this service as well. We look at designing funeral flowers as an important part of our flower ministry participating in the celebration from birth to death. Our Flower guild members often know the families or the deceased and are happy to be part of the celebration. Each week we schedule members who are on reserve for funerals or memorial services. We also will create special arrangements if the family chooses.
The families often choose to use the flowers that are on the altar from Sunday.

This particular design was created in memory of very special, active and beloved woman in our parish.
She loved white flowers. We call the design "On the Wings of Angels" because it gives the essence of angel. She had seen a similar altar we had done and requested it for her service.

Steps

1. Set up the mechanics and soak the Oasis.
2. Cover the base with Pittosporum and Leather Leaf.
3. Set the line with the Myrtle and line flowers.
4. Place the focal flowers in each of the three sections.
5. Spread the Roses evenly throughout the design.
6. Fill with the white Stock and Phlox.

Materials

Mechanics
1 Low Urn for center
4 Ceramic boxes on the sides
1 Large Oasis and 6 regular Oasis bricks

Greenery
2 Bunches Green Pittosporum
1 Bunch Myrtle
10 Stems Sword Fern
1 Bunch Leather Leaf

Flowers
Line: 20 Stems White Gladiolas
10 Stems White Snapdragons
5 Stems White Hybrid Delphinium

Focal: 10 Stems White Peonies
10 Stems White Lilies

Supporting: 25 Stems White Rose "Polo"
25 Stems Rose "Vendela"

Filler: 20 Stems White Stock
20 Stems White Phlox

Baptism Wreaths

Placing a simple wreath around the font is a special touch for baptismal services. We like to use delicate blooms that gently encircle the wreath. This soft pastel color palette is especially appropriate for baptisms for infants. It looks nice with this antique marble font.

Materials

Mechanics
One Oasis 18" wreath form
¼" Waterproof Tape
Sheet Moss

Greenery
½ Bunch Green Pittosporum
¼ Bunch Variegated Pittosporum
3 Stems Variegated English Boxwood
2 Stems Leafless Seeded Eucalyptus
Sheet Moss

Flowers
6 Stems Spray Rose "Porcelina"
8 Stems Light Pink Spray Carnations
10 Stems Lavender Scabiosa
10 Stems White Freesia
3 Stems Feverfew
5 Stems Blue Delphinium
½ Bunch Feverfew "Single Vegmo"

Steps

1. "Chamfer" the edge of the wreath (i.e. cut of hard edge at a slight diagonal All the way around.)
2. Wrap ¼" tape all the way around about 3" apart. Soak.
3. Green Oasis paying particular attention to covering middle section and edges. Leave gaps for flowers.
4. Place focal flowers (Spray Roses and Scabiosa in an even pattern going up and down).
5. Insert Spray Carns in between.
6. Insert Freesia allowing its tips to drape downwards.
7. Cut Delphinium into bits with two or three flowers each. Use to fill gaps.
8. Add a touch of Feverfew to soften.
9. Tuck Sheet Moss under to soften and cover edge of the wreath.

Thanksgiving Single Design

Thanksgiving is a harvest festival celebrated by cultures around the world since human prehistory. Humans have celebrated at harvest time as expression of gratitude. A simple basket of flowers surrounded by fruit and vegetables reflects the bounty of the season.
Thanksgiving arrangements are some of our favorite to create because we like to use different materials including fruits and vegetables mixed with fall grasses and dried materials. The chocolate brown Orchids contrast nicely to traditional fall flowers. The design can be made ahead with Mums and long-lasting flowers as it is often difficult to find volunteers to arrange the day before Thanksgiving.

Steps

1. Cut Oasis to fit basket. It does not need to fit edge to edge. Just enough to hold the flowers. Soak Oasis.
2. Lightly cover with greenery for a gentle rounded shape.
3. Insert line flowers (okra and millet)
4. Insert the focal Roses and cymbidiums. Cut cymbidiums in pieces to insert.
5. Fill with Carnations and fall materials, wheat, millet and fall leaves.
6. Add fruit if desired or surround with fruit and vegetables (See Basics for info on wiring)

Materials

Mechanics
Basket with plastic liner
Oasis to fit

Greenery
5 Stems Camellia
1 Bunch Leather Leaf
1 Bunch Salal
5 Stems Treated Fall Leaves
  (Yellow, Brown, Red)

Flowers
3 Stems Red Okra on Stem
5 Stems Millet "Pearl"
8 Stems Grass Millet Green "Foxtail"
6 Stems Millet Seeded
5 Stems Wheat
2 Stems Cymbidium Orchids "Chocolate"
3 Stems Rose "Leonidas"
8 Stems Rose "Espana"
3 Stems Orange Ranunculus
7 Stems Carnation "Merlot Crimson"
Collection of fruit and vegetables for base: acorn squash, butternut squash, apples, corn

Reception

Introduction

Churches are places of hospitality welcoming people and celebrating special events. The traditions vary from church to church. There are many occasions where the community comes together to welcome new members, to commemorate newly ordained clergy, to honor retiring clergy, to celebrate baptisms or the life of a departed member.

Parishioners often bring food for the gatherings. Church Flower Guilds can help with these celebrations by creating floral designs to serve as centerpieces. The special touch of flowers created by church members adds a sense of the community coming together. Church parish halls are often large and cavernous requiring lots of flowers and greenery. Arrangements of this size would be expensive to purchase commercially. Flower Guilds can learn how to create reception flowers for these occasions. This next section shows some examples of these types of centerpiece designs, which could be used on a buffet or a centerpiece for the gathering. We begin with a basic smaller arrangement and move to a grand urn design for a larger space. Basic recipes are given that can be altered to fit the space or colors desired.

Reception
Grand Urn "Stained Glass" Palette

This design uses a color scheme we often use because it is based upon the colors of stained glass. When you examine our stained glass there are lots of blues, reds and yellows. We add white to the design to lighten it up and make the other colors pop. Since purple is the color of a Cathedral, we often put a touch of purple in these designs. The limelight Hydrangea was from the church grounds.

Steps

1. Find plastic liner that fits the top of the urn.
2. Use largest solid piece of Oasis that fits the dish. We used a designer block.
3. Cover the Oasis with chicken wire cap and tape as shown in Basics Chapter.
4. Cover base with Pittosporum or other low greens.
5. Set a tall straight piece of greenery directly in the center. Step back and check that it is in the center.
6. Place three slightly shorter pieces of greenery around the center leaving space.
7. Place the lower draping materials around the bottom creating a skirt.
8. Use the remaining greenery including Aucuba, Salal and Leather Leaf to build between the top and bottom in a radial fashion.
9. Insert line flowers starting with the largest ones (i.e. Gladiolas) in the center and 4 surrounding the top one.
10. Place the lower line flowers evenly around the bottom.
11. Build between with line flowers: Add four line flowers on the next row. Add four more in between on the next row and so on.
12. Place red Roses starting at top and working downward in a zig zag pattern. Start with red Roses. Then work free spirits in between.
13. Fill gaps with Hydrangea and Stock.
14. Add Craspedia for pops of yellow to carry yellow through the design. It is best to group the Craspedia.

Materials

Mechanics
- 15" Round Plastic Dish
- 1 Grande Urn 18" Wide x 23" High Dimensions
- 1 Oasis Designer Size
- 1/2" Waterproof Tape

Greenery.
- Line: 4 Stems Sassanqua (tall and straight)
- Drape: 4 Stems Sassanqua (draping pieces)
- 5 Pieces Glossy Abelia
- Base: 1 Bunches Green Pittosporum
- 5 Stems Aucuba
- 5 Stems Tea Olive
- 1 Bunch Leather Leaf

Flowers
- Line: 5 Stems Yellow Gladiolas
- 10 Stems White Snapdragons
- 9 Stems Hybrid Blue Delphinium
- 10 Stems Purple Larkspur
- Focal:
- 15 Stems Red Roses "Corazon"
- 12 Stems Rose "Free Spirit"
- Filler:
- 10 Stems Hydrangea "Limelight"
- 10 Stems White Stock
- Special:
- 20 Stems Craspedia "Billy Balls"

Hint 1
Use a turntable under your design if at all possible.

Hint 2
Keep checking your shape from all sides to make sure it is even and centered.

Hint 3
Even placement of line flowers and focal flowers will create a strong shape. Adding filler flower and special bits will soften the look.

Reception — Small Centerpiece

This small simple design can be used for many occasions. This bright yellow palette is complemented by the pops of bright blue and green.

Steps

Find plastic liner that fits the top of the urn.
1. Use Grande brick with a wedge on each side.
2. Cover the Oasis with chicken wire cap and tape as shown in Basics Chapter.
3. Cover base with Pittosporum or other low greens. Set the center greenery directly in the center.
4. Step back and check.
5. Place three tall slightly smaller pieces of greenery around the center leaving space.
6. Insert line flowers starting with the Snapdragons in the center and 3 surrounding the top one.
7. Place the lower line flowers evenly around the bottom.
8. Build between with line flowers: Add four line flowers on the next row.
9. Place Lilies around middle third of design in an up-and-down pattern.
10. Alternate bright green Mums around Lilies.
11. Use Calla Lilies to reinforce shape and drape.
12. Fill gaps with Phlox and Stock.
13. Add Craspedia for pops of yellow to carry yellow through the design.
14. Add thistle for interest at level where it can be seen.
15. Finish bottom of design by creating a skirt around the bottom with draping Leather Leaf and other garden materials.

Materials

Mechanics
- 11" Lomey Dish
- 1 Compote or Small Urn
- 1 Oasis Designer Size
- 1/4" Waterproof Tape

Greenery
- Line: 3 Stems Camellia
- Base: 1 Bunches Green Pittosporum
  - 5 Stems Aucuba
  - 6 Stems Dwarf Yedda Hawthorne
  - 1 Bunch Leather Leaf
  - ½ Bunch Variegated Boxwood

Flowers
- Line: 7 Yellow Snapdragons
  - 10 Stems White Larkspur
  - 10 Stems Delphinium Sea Waltz
- Focal: 6 Stems Yellow Asiatic Lilies
  - Supporting
  - 8 Stems Yellow Calla Lilies
- Filler: 7 Stems Green Button Mums
  - 7 Stems Green Athos Mum
  - 10 Stems Pale Yellow Stock
  - 8 Stems White Phlox
- Interest: 10 Stems Craspedia
  - 1 Bunch Blue Thistle
    (Eryngium "Deep Blue Jackpot")

Basic Small Centerpiece Recipe
- 1 Bunches Line Greenery
- 2 Bunches Basic Greenery
- 2-3 Bunches Line Flowers
- 1 Bunch Focal Flower
- 1-2 Bunches Supporting Flower
- 1-2 Bunches Filler
- 1-2 Bunches Interest
  (if budget permits!)

Hint
Keep it soft and loose by adding less dense flowers such as Phlox and Delphinium.

Reception — Blush Centerpiece

Lots of fully open, blush toned Roses make a lovely design for a memorial reception for a woman. We used a variety of soft pink Roses leftover from the altar design.

Steps

1. Cut and fit Oasis to dish with grande side in center and a wedge on each side.
2. Cover the Oasis with chicken wire cap and tape as shown in Basics Chapter.
3. Cover base with Pittosporum and Variegated Boxwood.
4. Set the center greenery directly in the center. Step back and check.
5. Place four Snapdragons: one in the center and three surrounding it.
6. Place three Snapdragons around middle and three around the bottom in between the middle ones.
7. Reinforce the line with Peach Stock.
8. Start inserting Roses by type placing in up and down pattern spreading evenly throughout the design. Repeat with each type of Rose.
9. Use the Carnations to reinforce the Roses tucking about 2' deeper.
10. Insert the Cleyera branches so that their glossy leaves can be seen.
11. Fill gaps with filler flowers.

Materials

Mechanics
11" Lomey Dish
1 22" Tall Brass Compote
1 Oasis Grande Size
½ Oasis Split into two wedges
1/2" Waterproof Tape

Greenery
1 Bunch Pittosporum
1 Bunch Variegated Boxwood
5 Stems Cleyera

Flowers
Line: 1 Bunch Pink Snapdragons
5 Stems Peach Stock

Focal: 5 Stems Rose "Pink Mondial"
12 Stems Rose "Mother of Pearl"
7 Stems Rose "Quicksand"

Supporting: 12 Stems Carnation "Babylon"

Filler: 10 Stems Orlaya
10 Stems White Phlox
10 Stems White and light pink alstromeria

Hint
Roses and Alstroemeria should be fully open for this design. Start opening them three or four days ahead!

Flower Festivals

Flower Festivals are community celebrations of flowers. Churches make ideal locations for Flower Festivals because there are so many interesting areas to decorate. The concept is that different areas of the church are decorated with flowers by its Flower Guild, other churches, garden clubs, flower lovers or any combination of these groups.

They can be held annually or on special occasions. Educational programs can be offered as part of the festival. One or more speakers are invited to present a demonstration of flower arranging or a lecture on flower related topics. Sometimes there are hands on workshops offered in conjunction with the program. Members of the community are invited to attend to see the array of floral designs. A fee may be charged for admission or for the educational programs to help pay for the cost of the flowers and speakers or for donations to a charity.

We encourage churches to offer a flower festival. Small churches as well as large ones can make a festival happen. It is a joyful experience for volunteers and visitors alike.

Cathedral Flower Festival:
At our Cathedral, we have an Flower Festival which occurs in conjunction with our annual Antiques Show each winter. Each year a different charity is selected to receive the net proceeds of the funds from the show.
We have over 20 churches and garden clubs that come together to decorate the Cathedral. The setup day is an exciting bundle of activity as over 100 volunteers work to flower the show with their floral designs.
Within six hours the space is completely transformed. The Flower Festival adds a breath of life and the hope of spring as visitors come through the Antiques Show and Flower Festival. We call the Friday of the show "Flower Friday" and have flower related speakers and programs during the day.

Here are some photos from The Cathedral Antiques Show and Flower Festival.

Flowers by (clockwise):
Oatleaf Flower and Garden,
St. Luke's Episcopal Church, Habersham Garden Club,
Flower Demonstration, All Saints Episcopal Church,
Druid Hills Garden Club, Iris Garden Club.
Page 4: Cary Lide on behalf of A.G. Rhodes - 2018 Antiques Show Benificary.

So many dedicated and talented people have been involved in the production of this book.

Special thanks

To God, for providing me with the skills and opportunities which have brought so much joy and for the incredible people who I have met along this flower path.

To the Cathedral of St. Philip for the use of its glorious space and to Dean Sam Candler, George Maxwell, Wallace Marsh, and David Rocchio and to the entire staff who helped in countless ways.

To the Cathedral of St. Philip Flower Guild members, who lovingly toiled to create many of the flowers in this book for their dedication, enthusiasm and talents. For my guild co-chairs over the years for their endless support, inspiration, and beautiful design skills including Jill Brennan, Victoria Denson, Josh Borden, Darrin Ellis May, and Grace Foster. Many hands took part in the creation of the designs in the book and all the flowers at the Cathedral.
It is difficult to thank everyone individually and I am sure I have missed some. It takes a team and I appreciate everyone. I am especially grateful to all the lead designers who have helped to create designs in this book:
Victoria Denson (Pentecost, Easter Baskets), Morgan Ellington (Spring Fresh Wedding), Kay Ottley (Easter) Darrin Ellis May (Radial Design in Blue, Easter Pulpit and Christmas Draping Ivy), Caroline Gilham (Caroline's Cascade), Terry Morris (Easter Garland), Harriet Segars (Spring Fresh Wedding, Golden Garden Greenery and Easter Garland), Josh Borden (Reception Introduction), Saye Sutton (Classic Christmas and Kneeling Altars), Terry Vawter (On the Wings of Angels).

To all my teachers and friends including Tyler Gresham, Hitomi Gilliam, Gudrun Cottenier, Tom De Wilde, Rob Plattel, Gail Johnson, Kay Ottley, and Josh Borden. Caroline Gilham who has taught and inspired me to use wonderful garden-grown materials and lent her advice and wisdom to the development of the beautiful grounds at the Cathedral. To my friends in the flower industry from whom I am continually learning.

To my incredibly talented and dedicated staff, including Mary Brannon, Virginia Parker, Virginia Reticker, Laura Caroline Iarocci and Kori Horvath. They have been with me through photo shoots, preparing flowers, cleaning up and arranging ... whatever it has taken to get the job done. I am especially grateful to Virginia Parker who has stood with me to the very last day of completion. I could not have done it without your support, advice and assistance!

To Tessa Marie Swarthout, my principal photographer who has been with me through the entire year of shooting. Her attention to detail, artistic vision and stamina got us through many a long photoshoot. To our special Cathedral photographers for their beautiful imagery including Matt Yung, Anna & Spencer, Rustic White and Sandra & Greg.

To my friends and reps at Cut Flower Wholesale and Halls Atlanta Wholesale who never tire in answering my questions about availability, delivery, and the care and keeping of flowers.
I am so appreciative of the knowledge you share about new varieties. Thank you for procuring the flowers used in this book many of which were out of season. Kevin Criswell, Scott Shepard, Mike Balsnick, Rene Ten Braak and Steve Haywood -- you are the best stems in the bunch.

To my husband, Joe for his continuous support, love and guidance through this flower journey. For all the branches you have collected, lunches brought and errands run.
To my children Alex, Allison and Laura Caroline and my parents, Marilyn and Terry for encouraging me and helping me to pursue my passion for flowers.

Author
Laura Iarocci
www.faithflowers.com
flowerguild@FaithFlowers.com
1183 Virginia Avenue, NE
Atlanta, Georgia 30306
Telephone: 404-922-8298
FB: FaithFlowers
Instagram: FaithFlowersATL

All photography in the book was created by
Tessa Marie Studios (tessamarie.com)
with the exception of the following:
Matt Yung Photography: p. 3, 4, 41 (BR), 91, 99, 100, 103, 105, 140-141
Anna and Spencer Photography: p. 77 (TL), 78, 86 (BL), 87, 89 (BL)
Emily Dean Photography: p. 75
Ross Henderson: p. 79 (BL)
Rustic White Photography: p. 77 (BR), 82, 83, 88 (BR)
Picture This! Sandra and Greg: p. 84, 85, 142
Rene Brock Photojournalist: p. 81
Decisive Moment: p. 86 (TR)
Two Chics photography: p. 86 (BR), p. 88 (BL)

Layout
www.groupvandamme.eu

Published by
Stichting Kunstboek bvba
Legeweg 165
B-8020 Oostkamp, Belgium
T: +32 50 46 19 10
info@stichtingkunstboek.com
www.stichtingkunstboek.com

ISBN 978-90-5856-588-4
D/2018/6407/02
NUR 421

Printed in the EU

All rights reserved. No part of this book
may be reproduced, stored in a database
or a retrieval system, or transmitted, in any form
or by any means, electronically, mechanically,
by print, microfilm or otherwise without prior
permission from the Publisher.

© Faith Flowers 2018
© Stichting Kunstboek 2018

A Special Invitation
We invite you to join us in creating
beautiful flowers for churches.
To become part of this greater world
of church flowers, please join
the Faith Flowers Guild.
Please let us know of your interest
at info@faithflowers.com.

FAITH FLOWERS
STUDIO & SCHOOL